Contents

Chapter 1
Basic Tools

Getting started

Jasc Paint Shop Pro is a powerful art package which you can use to paint, write text, retouch photos and make images ready for the web. After only a few lessons you will be creating amazing pictures and effects.

Let's get started!

- Load Jasc Paint Shop Pro 8. You can do this in one of two ways:

- Either double-click the Paint Shop Pro icon
- or click **Start** at the bottom left of the screen, then click **Programs**. When the programs pop up click:

If this is the first time you have used Paint Shop Pro after installing it, you will see a window asking you to select the file types that will be associated with Paint Shop Pro.

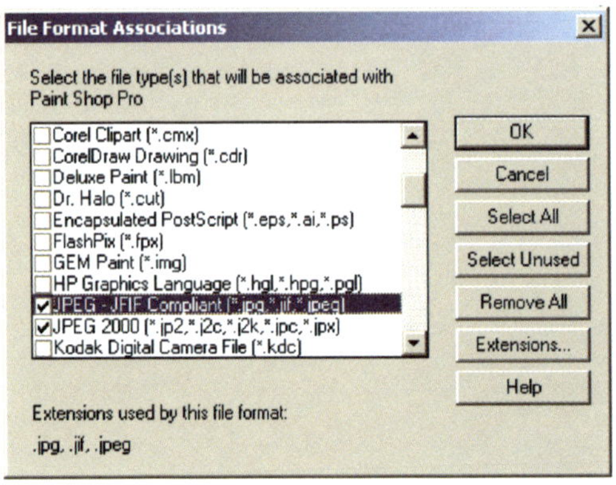

Figure 1.1: Setting File Format associations

You can either just click **OK** to accept the default settings, or you can select other file formats such as the JPEG file format.

- Click **OK**.

Tip:

When you associate a file format with Paint Shop Pro, a file in that format will open in Paint Shop Pro when you double-click it in the Windows desktop.

You can change these associations later by selecting **File, Preferences, File Format Associations.**

The Opening Screen

- Your screen will look like the one below:

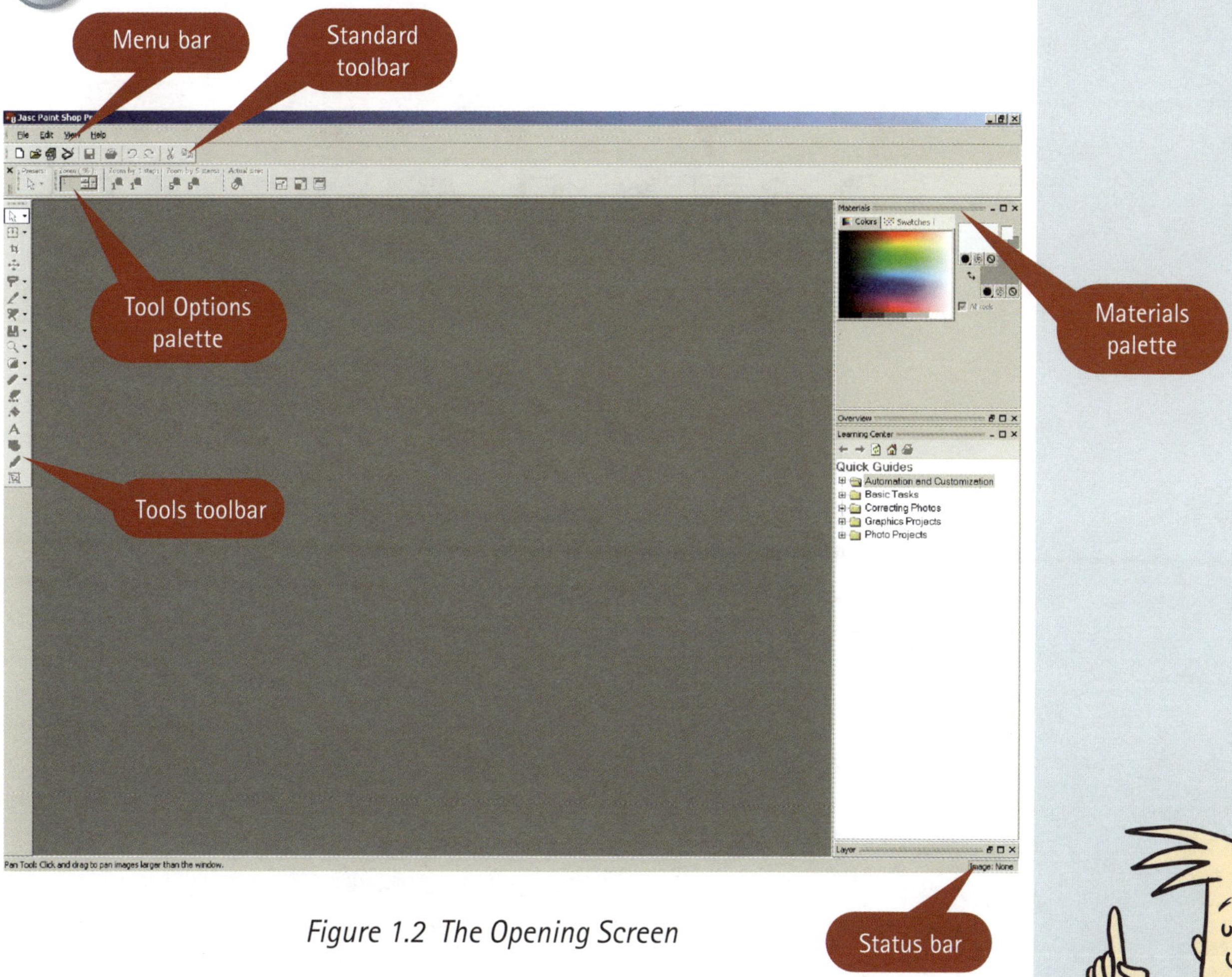

Figure 1.2 The Opening Screen

- At the top of the screen is the **Menu bar**. The **Help** option on this menu is useful for getting extra information on a particular topic.

- Just below the **Menu bar** is the **Standard toolbar**. This has icons which may be clicked instead of choosing common options from the menu.

- The **Tool Options palette** may be visible under the Standard toolbar. This changes depending on what tool is selected.

- Down the left side of the screen is the **Tools toolbar**. This allows you to use a great variety of effects, distortions, paint brushes and spray cans to dramatically enhance your pictures.

- Down the right side you'll see a number of **palettes** which we will look at later. The **Learning Centre** has a useful **Quick Guide** to help you with any problems you might have.

- The **Status Bar** gives you image size and cursor position information.

Tip:

Some of the palettes are minimised in the screenshot. The palettes may look different on your screen if they are not minimised.

Toolbars and Palettes

Some of the tools on the Standard toolbar such as New, Open, Save and Print should be familiar to you.

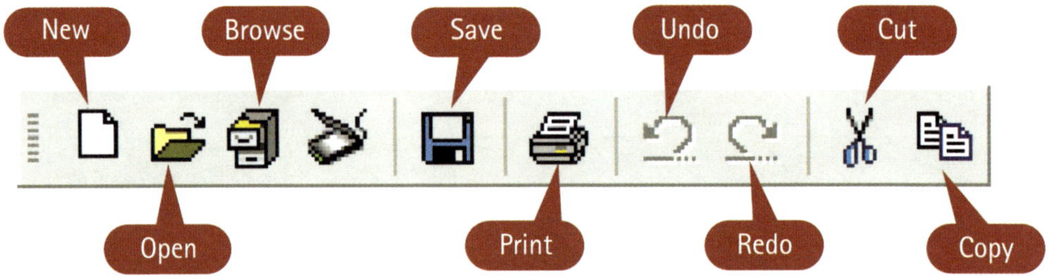

Figure 1.3

Right-click anywhere in the toolbar, and a pop-up window will appear. Choose Palettes. You will see options to open or close different palettes, which is especially useful if you don't have much room on your screen.

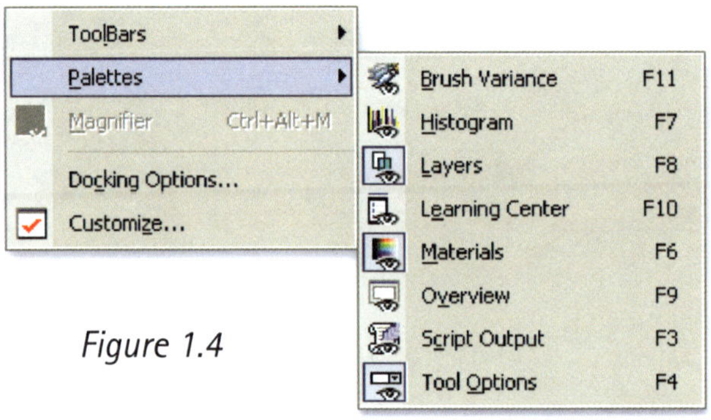

Figure 1.4

Close all the palettes except the Materials and Tool Options palettes.

Now you can close some of the toolbars.

Right-click a toolbar again, and this time select ToolBars. Close all the toolbars except Standard, Status and Tools.

Figure 1.5

This should make the screen look a lot less complicated and a little friendlier! You can open the other toolbars and palettes when you need them.

Creating a new image

- Choose File, New, and the New Image window appears.
- Set the Width and Height to 500 pixels and the resolution to 72 pixels (dots) per inch.
- In the Image Characteristics make sure the Raster Background is checked.
- The Colour depth default is set to 16 Million Colours. Leave this.
- Click in the Color box. Another window will open and, using either the colour box or the wheel, choose a bright red.

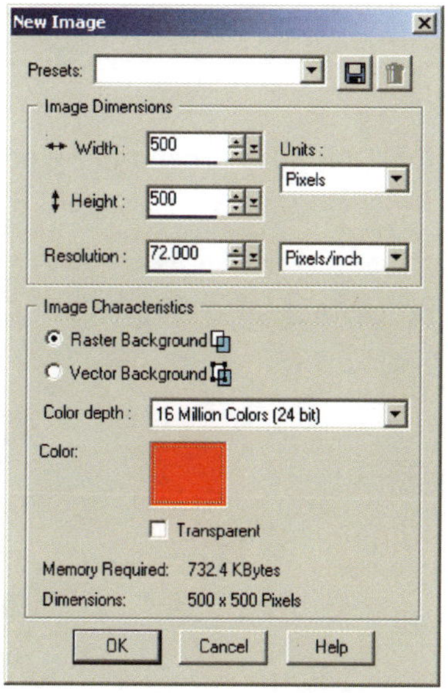

Figure 1.6: New Image settings

- Click OK.

Your screen will look like this:

Figure 1.7: Red Image

Tip:

72 dpi (dots per inch) is the norm for most computer screens. But if you need to print something it may need to be a higher resolution.

Note:

At top of the canvas the Title bar displays the name of the file (which will change as soon as we save the file), the size as a percent and the layer currently selected.

Tip:

It is important to save your work at regular intervals and to be sure that you do not lose too much if something unexpected happens, such as a power cut or Artistic Tantrum!

We will save our new image.

- Click File on the Menu bar and select Save As. Under File Name save it as Floating and ensure the Save as Type is on the setting Paint Shop Pro Image. Click Save.

- Now let's go ahead and explore Paint Shop Pro's possibilities on our new red background.

The Tools toolbar

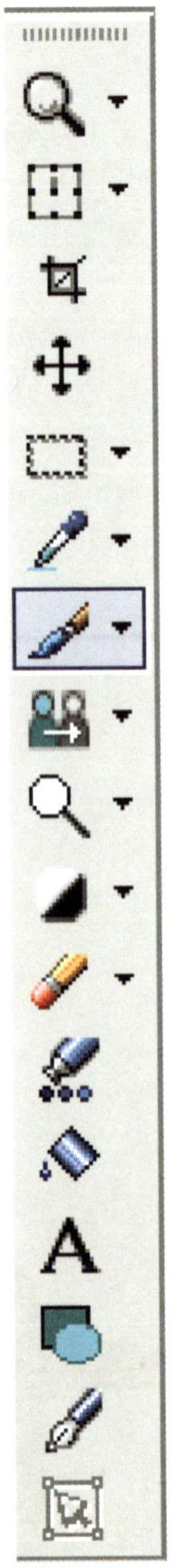

Zoom tool (alternates with Pan tool)
Deform tool
Crop tool
Mover tool
Selection tool (also Freehand Selection and Magic Wand)
Dropper tool
Paint Brush tool (also Airbrush and Warp Brush)
Clone Brush
Dodge Brush
Lighten/Darken Brush
Eraser tool
Picture Tube tool
Flood Fill tool
Text tool
Preset Shape tool
Pen tool
Object Selection tool

Figure 1.8: The Tools toolbar

A tool button with a small down-arrow on the right side includes several tools. Click the down-arrow to choose an alternative tool.

The Tools toolbar includes some tools that we do not need to know at this point, but we will look at some of them in detail now.

The Paint Brush

The Paint Brush is a painting tool. The width and shape of the brush, the amount and density of the paint on the brush, and how it behaves all depend on settings in the Tool Options palette.

Left-click the Paint Brush icon. If you click the down-arrow you will see there are two other options, an Airbrush and a Warp Brush. (If the Paint Brush does not appear on your Tools toolbar, but the Airbrush or Warp Brush does, then click the down-arrow and select Paint Brush.)

To choose the **Paint Brush** you can simply press the **'B'** key on your keyboard.

Figure 1.9: Extra tools

The Tool Options palette

If the Tool Options palette is not displayed on your screen, click View on the Menu bar and choose Palettes, Tool Options. This palette has different options depending on which tool is selected. It will 'dock' under the Standard toolbar.

Enter the settings as shown in Figure 1.10.

Tip:

You can right-click any of the light grey menu areas and find more options to open and close **Palettes** and **Toolbars**.

Figure 1.10: The Tool Options palette for the Paint Brush tool

Try writing your name and also try drawing circles and putting a dot in the middle.

Try changing the Size options.

To change the colour of the brush move your mouse cursor over the Colour Square in the Materials palette and your cursor will automatically change to a Dropper icon.

As you move the Dropper icon over the available colours, the selected colour appears in the box attached to your Dropper icon.

> **Tip:**
> Reducing Opacity is like adding water to your paintbrush – some of the background shows through.

Try doodling on the screen with different colours.

Now try changing the Hardness in the Tool Options palette.
Try painting a circle with 100 percent hardness, and then decreasing by 20 percent steps down to 0 percent to see what happens. Do the same with the Opacity.

Zoom tool

Click the Zoom tool (the top icon on the Tools toolbar) and you will see a new Tool Options palette and a series of options.

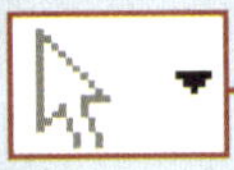

(If you cannot see the Zoom tool, click the down-arrow next to the Pan tool and select Zoom.)

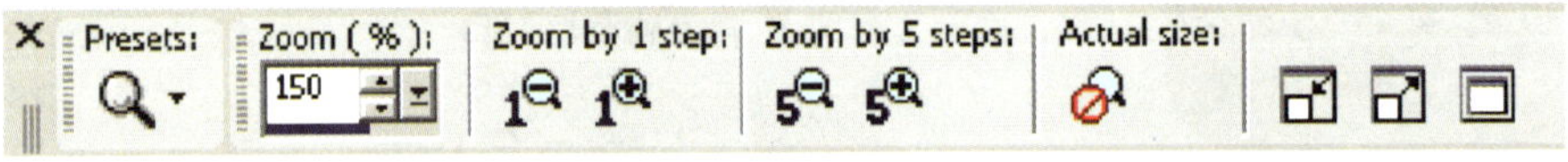

Figure 1.11: The Zoom Tool Options palette

> **Tip:**
> If you have a wheel on your mouse you can automatically zoom in and out.

Click Zoom by 1 step, and try zooming in and out until you find a size you like working at.

To return your image to the original size, click the Actual size icon.

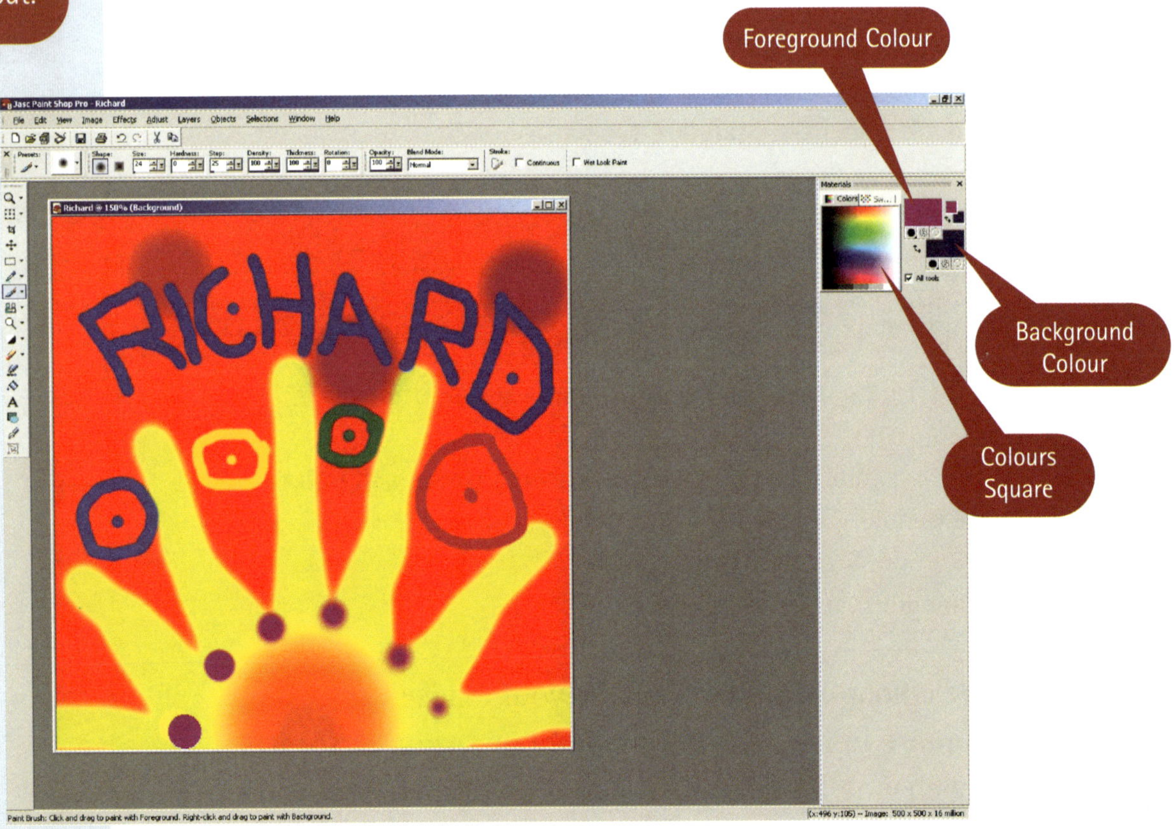

Figure 1.12

Foreground and background colours

When you run the dropper over the Colours Square and left-click, you are selecting a new foreground colour. If you right-click instead, you select a new background colour. The colours appear in the two swatches at the top of the Materials palette.

You can paint with the background colour by dragging with the right mouse button instead of the left. Try it!

Tip:

You can swap foreground and background colours in the two swatches by clicking the two-headed arrow between them.

The Dropper tool

If you want to paint another line with exactly the same colour you used, say for the R in Figure 1.12, you need the Dropper tool. Left-click it and then left-click the R in your canvas. Select the Paint Brush tool and the foreground colour changes to the colour of this line.

Or, you can right-click with the Dropper tool to change the background colour. Then select the Paint Brush tool again, right-click and paint with the Background colour.

Undoing mistakes

If you don't like the last line you painted, you can undo it by clicking the Undo button.

Or, you can undo a whole lot of strokes using Edit, Command History. This brings up a window like Figure 1.13:

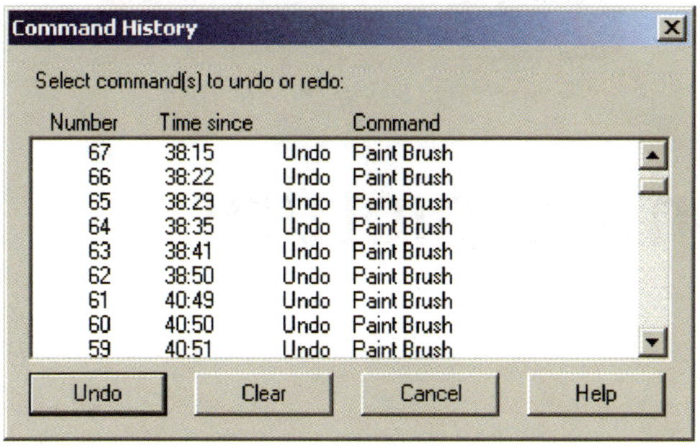

Figure 1.13: Undoing commands

You cannot undo just command number 60, for example. You can only undo every command back to a selected number.

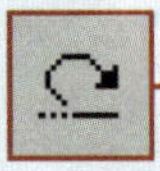

You can redo the commands by clicking the Redo button on the Standard toolbar.

- Select File, Close to close the canvas – no need to save.

The Airbrush

The Airbrush is almost the same as the Paint Brush and you choose your colours in the same way. The main difference is that if you hold the airbrush in one spot, more colour is deposited.

- Open a new canvas.
- Select the Airbrush (it shares a spot with the Paint Brush tool, so click the down-arrow next to the Paint Brush tool if it is not displayed in the Tools toolbar) and set the options as shown below.

- It has much softer edges like a spray would be. Have a go with it. Spray circles over each other to make a rainbow after a crash effect!

Tip:

Remember: when colouring in, you can left-click for foreground colour and right-click for background colour. Try reducing **Opacity** for a softer effect.

Figure 1.14: Using the Airbrush

Copying a picture

You can make a copy of your picture and have both copies open.

- Right-click in the Title bar of your picture and select Copy. Then right-click again and select Paste.
- Select Paste As New Image.

The Picture Tube

The Picture Tube is probably the most fun tool in the whole package. Let's have a go with it. Click the Picture Tube tool.

You will notice first that the Tool Options palette has completely changed. Let's assume that the picture you now have is a blancmange. Let's find some sweets to garnish it.

- Have a look at the new Tool Options palette.

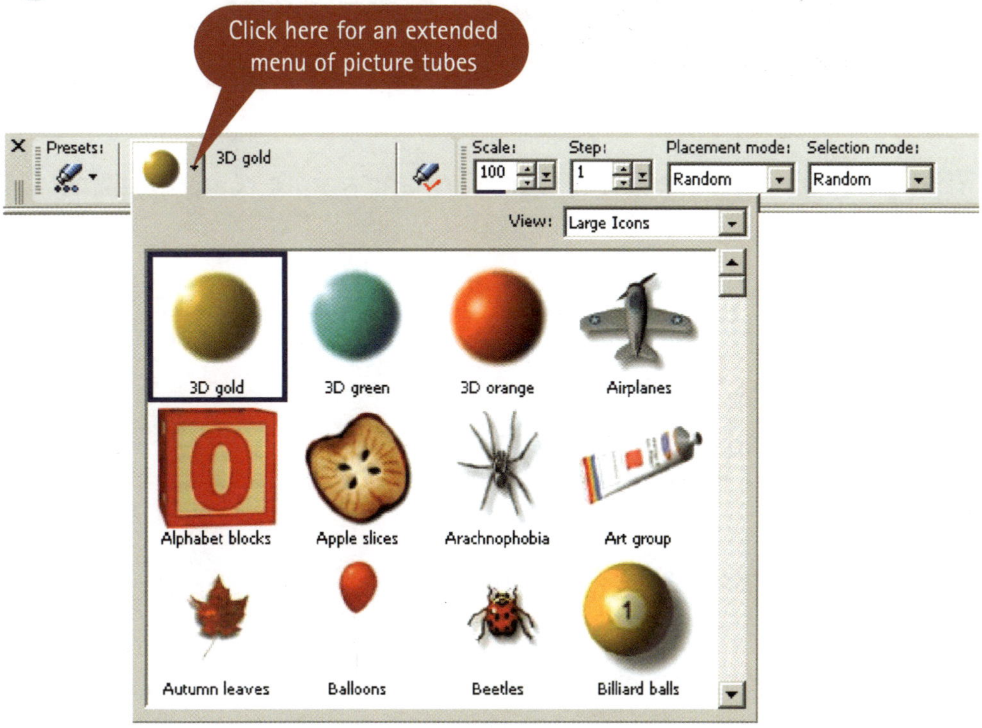

Figure 1.15

Tip:

Change the **Scale** and **Step** options and see what happens.

- Click the down-arrow to open the extended menu of picture tubes and select a tube you wish to use. I suggest using Candy corn, Sweets and Jellybeans.
- Once a tube has been selected, click your cursor over your canvas as many times as you wish to produce the image.
- Go back to the menu to select another tube and repeat the process.
- If you don't like the arrangement of sweets you can either go to File and press Revert which loads your last saved canvas or use Edit, Undo which will take you back one step.

After arranging the sweets in the first picture, try using the Balloon and Metallic Streamers picture tubes in the second picture.
Try adding the balloons and streamers attached to the string with Scale 25% and then more balloons at 50%, 75% and 100% to create a feeling of depth.

Figure 1.16

That's it! You can now save your work and you're ready to print your favourite one.

Printing

From the File menu select Print.

Of course you will need a colour printer to make it worth printing the work of art you have created!

Before you click Print, look carefully at the preview on the right of the window. This shows you what your picture will look like when printed. You can check the appropriate boxes to change the orientation of the paper or even the size of your picture on the page.

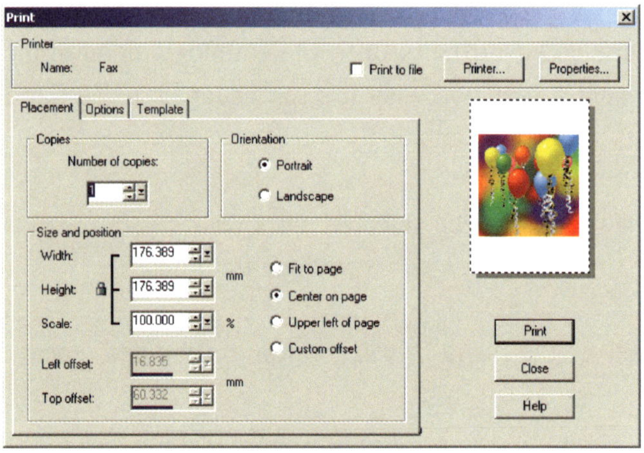

Figure 1.17: The Page Setup dialogue box

You can now click the Print button.

Close both images and exit Paint Shop Pro by clicking the Close icon in the top right-hand corner or by selecting File, Exit.

Chapter 2
Selections

Making selections

A selection masks off an area so that you can paint it, move it, copy it or fill it with special effects.

There are three basic tools for making selections.

 The Selection tool

 The Freehand Selection tool

 The Magic Wand tool

The Selection tool

The Selection tool enables you to make selections using different shapes. We'll try it out.

- Open a new canvas with dimensions 500 x 500 pixels, resolution 72 pixels per inch, 16 million colours and a white background.
- Make sure the Title bar says Image1 100% (Background). If it says Image1 60% (Background) you are 'zoomed out' and you will have a very small working area.
- In that case click the Zoom tool on the Tools toolbar. Then click the Actual Size (1:1) button in the Zoom Tool Options palette.
- Click the Selection tool.

Tip:

The **Zoom** tool shares the top spot in the **Tools** toolbar with the **Pan** tool. A quick way to zoom is to press **Z** on the keyboard.

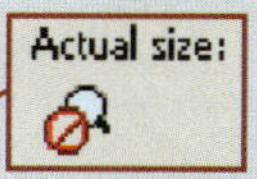

Drawing with the Selection tool

The Tool Options palette for the Selection tool should already be open. If it is not, right-click the Selection tool, click on Palettes and in there find Tool Options.

- In the Tool Options palette, click the arrow in the Selection Type box and you will see that you can make selections of various shapes. Make the Selection type Circle. Leave Feather as 0 and Anti-alias selected.

Figure 2.1: The Selection Tool Options palette

- Click on the canvas and draw out a circle. The circle expands from its centre as you drag.

- Draw a second circle, and you will see that the first one disappears.

- Select the Flood Fill tool. Select a green foreground colour by moving the cursor over the available colours in the Materials palette until you have a nice bright green in the colour swatch. Then left-click.

- Click in the selected circle and the area floods with green.

- Now click the Selection tool again and in the Tool Options palette, change the selection shape to a rounded rectangle.

- Draw a rectangle – this time it draws from a corner, not the centre. Use the Airbrush tool to fill it roughly with blue.

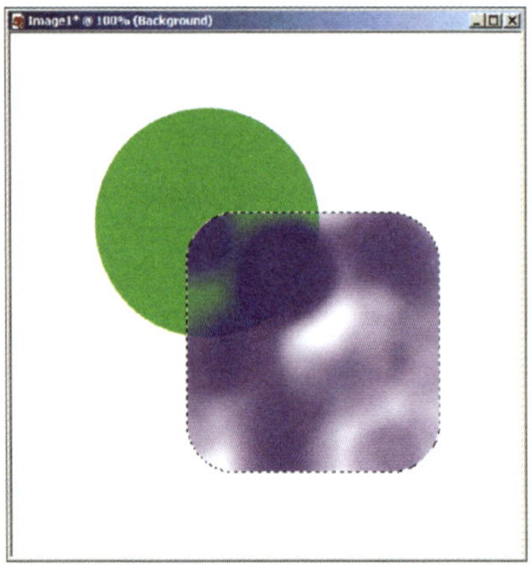

Figure 2.2: Selecting and filling shapes

Tip:

Don't start the rectangle inside the circle or you will select the circle and move it, exposing the current background colour. Just click the Undo icon if you go wrong.

Tip:

The black and white border around a selection is called a marquee. Sometimes it is referred to as the "marching ants".

Copying and pasting a selection

Close that canvas by clicking the X on the title bar, and now open another canvas 700 pixels wide and 500 high, with a white background, the same as the last one.

Tip:

Use an opacity of about 10 and airbrush lightly with green.

You are going to create a flag.

- Click the Selection tool and choose a triangle, drawing from the top right across to bottom left of your canvas.
- Flood Fill the triangle with yellow, and then draw a green pattern in the yellow triangle using the airbrush.
- To deselect the triangle, click the Selection tool again and right-click on the canvas.
- Choose Star 2 from the Selection Tool Options palette and draw a star in the white area to the right of your coloured triangle. Flood Fill it with blue.
- From the Edit menu select Copy or click the Copy button.

- From the Edit menu select Paste. In the submenu click Paste As New Selection. The star is copied into the middle of the canvas.
- It will move with the cursor until you left-click. Move it to approximately where you want it. You can fine-tune the position of the star by clicking the Mover tool and dragging the star.

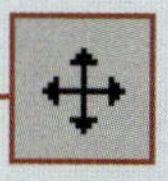

- Repeat the Paste operation twice more to paste two more blue stars. Move them to the positions shown below.
- Airbrush the last star with a selection of green.

Figure 2.3

You can clear all selections now.

- From the Selections menu choose Select None.

Tip:

Ctrl-D is a shortcut to Deselect All.

The Magic Wand tool

The Magic Wand tool allows you to select an area of a particular colour. You can set the Tolerance level so that colours which are almost but not quite the same will be selected.

- Click the Magic Wand tool (it shares the same spot as the Selection tool you have been using) and then click in the blue star at the bottom left.
- Change its colour to red.

Figure 2.4: Selecting with the Magic Wand tool

Setting the Tolerance level

Suppose you want to select the triangle. We will experiment with setting the Tolerance level of the Magic Wand.

- In the Tool Options for the Magic Wand, set the Tolerance level to 0.
- Click in the patterned triangle. Probably only a small portion of it will be selected.
- Keep increasing the Tolerance level and clicking in the triangle. Remember to deselect after each try.

When you have set the Tolerance level sufficiently high, the whole triangle will be selected when you click in it.

Adding selections

Now suppose you wanted to select the stars in addition to the triangle already selected. You add to selections by keeping the **Shift** key pressed while you make another selection.

- Keep the **Shift** key pressed and click in the stars.
- Select the white background as well. Then pick the **Airbrush**, set Size to **150**, Hardness to **0** and Opacity to **10%**.
- With the colour black selected, draw some soft lines vertically on your flag. Does it look as though it's flapping?

Figure 2.5: Flapping flag

- Save your picture if you want to, and close it.

The Freehand Selection tool

We will put some of our new skills to the test by drawing a pattern of flowers using the **Selection** and **Airbrush** tools.

- Open a new canvas, 500 pixels wide and high and specify a green background.
- Select the **Freehand Selection** tool (same spot as the **Magic Wand** tool) by clicking the tool icon and then place your cursor on the canvas. By dragging the cursor, draw a flower shape as in Figure 2.6. Don't forget you can have as many goes as you like to get it right. Just click **Selections** on the Menu bar and click on **Select None**. This will deselect the flower so you can draw another flower shape.

Tip:

You can also right-click in your selection to deselect it.

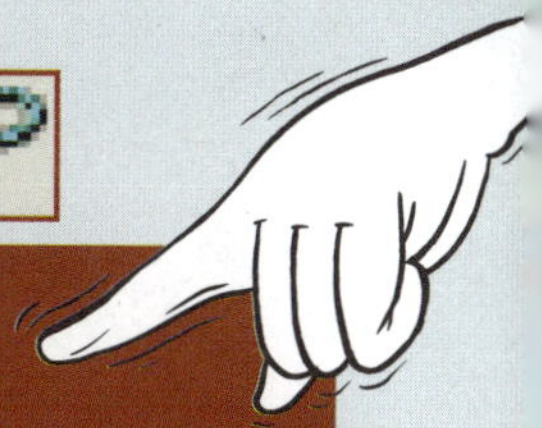

Tip:

Don't worry if you draw a wobbly line or spray the wrong colour, just undo using **Ctrl-Z** and try again. Practice makes perfect!

Figure 2.6

Now select the Airbrush tool. Move the cursor over the white area of the colour square and click. This will make the foreground white. Move the cursor over to the canvas, click and colour in the petals.

On the Selections menu click Select None. You can now draw the next part of your picture or draw the petals again.

In the Tools toolbar click on the Selection tool. In the Tool Options palette under Selection Type, select Circle.

Tip:

You can use the shortcut **Ctrl-D** to deselect.

Draw a circle in the middle of the flower. Click on the Airbrush and spray yellow in the circle selection. Deselect when you have finished colouring.

Figure 2.7

Hopefully you will have a flower like this! Now we are going to select the daisy and copy and paste it all over the canvas.

Pasting daisies

- Click the **Magic Wand** tool and select the yellow centre. Set the **Tolerance** on the **Tool Options** palette to **40**.

- Keep **Shift** held down while you click in the white part of the flower to select it. You may have to click in several petals if your yellow circle overlaps them.

- Click the **Copy** button to copy the selection. Then select **Edit**, **Paste** and choose **Paste As New Selection** from the submenu.

- Move the new daisy to where you want it.

- You can press **Ctrl-Y** to repeat the **Paste** operation as many times as you like, placing each daisy in a good position. When using **Ctrl-Y** the duplicate daisy appears over the last daisy pasted – you will need to drag it off and position it.

Figure 2.8

- You could try using a different background or just save your picture as **Flower Power**.

Try creating some other masterpieces!

Chapter 3 Cloning

Cloning

The Clone Brush is a very powerful tool and one of the most used implements in the world of professional photo retouchers and computer artists.

You'll need to spend some time playing around with it to understand how it works.

- Open a new canvas, 500 x 500 pixels and specify a purple background.

We are going to make a cartoon mad pig's face, something like the one in Figure 3.1. We will start with the pig's eyes.

Figure 3.1

- On the **Tools** toolbar, click the **Selection** tool and use the **Ellipse** selection to draw an ellipse roughly where I have drawn the pig's left eye.
- Choose the **Airbrush** and set the Brush Size to 100, and Opacity to 100. Spray the eye white.
- Then pick a darker blue, reduce the size of the **Airbrush** to 70 and set Hardness to 0 as you need a nice smooth edge. Carefully spray a shadow area at the bottom of the eye, I would set the Opacity to 30 before you start to spray the shadow so you can build up the colour without overdoing it.

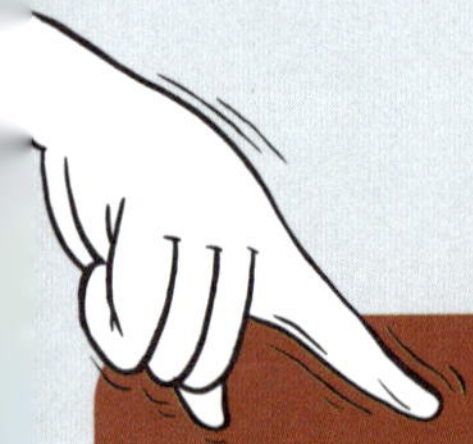

Note:

Opacity determines how thickly the paint is laid on: the higher the opacity, the thicker the paint.

Deselect (Ctrl-D) and use a circle Selection tool to draw the pupil. Colour it black, and think about where you are placing it because you could make a big difference to the character's expression!

Spray a white highlight over the pupil to give it a sparkle, make the Airbrush Size 40 and Opacity 100, and just give it one burst of highlight.

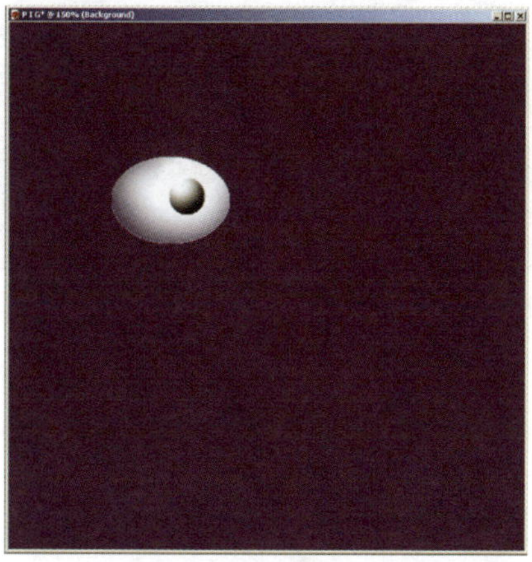

Figure 3.2

Deselect all.

Tip:

Remember you can press **Ctrl-Z** or use the **Undo** button to undo an action and try again!

Using the Clone Brush tool

Using the Clone Brush tool you can paint an exact copy of any part of an image, either on a new canvas or on another part of the same canvas.

There are three stages to using the Clone Brush tool:

- Set the Tool Options.
- Activate the Clone Brush by right-clicking on the image you want to clone.
- Position the cursor where you want to start copying. Left-click at that position and you will see a cross-hair on the original image to show exactly what portion is being copied. Drag the cursor to start copying.

Now give it a go!

Tip:

This tool can only be used on 16 million colour and greyscale images.

Click the Clone Brush tool and set the Tool Options as shown in Figure 3.3.

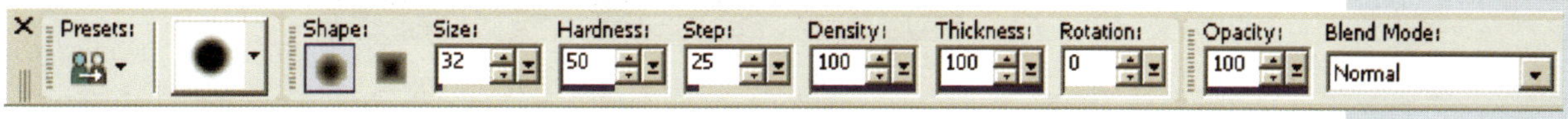

Figure 3.3

If the eye is in the wrong position this will give you a chance to practise moving a selection.

- Right-click somewhere in the pig's eye to activate the **Clone Brush**.
- Position the cursor on the right side of the face and start dragging it in small circles to clone the eye.

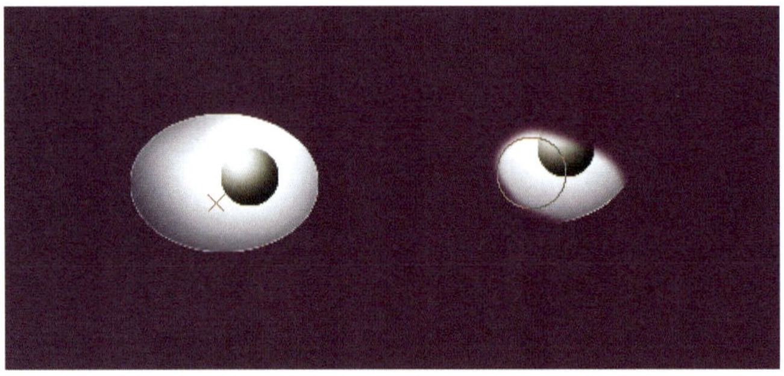

Figure 3.4: Starting to clone the eye

- Finish cloning the eye.

Moving a selection

The eye in Figure 3.4 is too high, and needs to be moved.

When the whole eye is selected, the **Selection** tool changes shape to that of the **Mover** tool as it passes over the selection. If you move the eye now by dragging it, it will leave behind a 'hole' in the background colour. Try it as follows:

- Use the **Magic Wand** to select the white part of the right eye. Then hold down **Shift** while you select the pupil.
- Now move the eye. You should see something like Figure 3.5.

Don't forget you can change the magic wand Tolerance so you can more easily select the gradients.

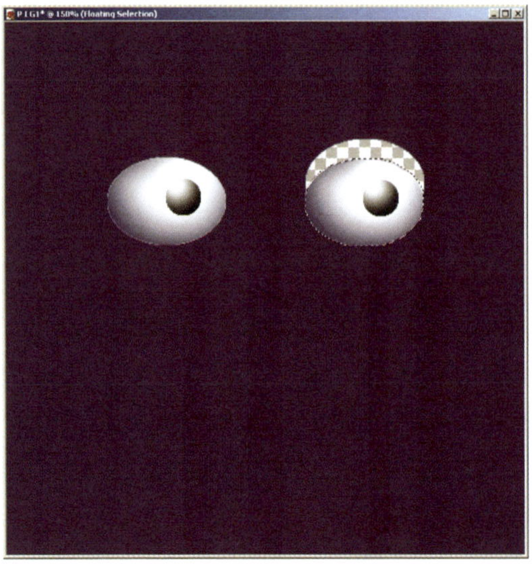

Figure 3.5: Moving a selection

From the **Selections** menu choose **Invert**. Check **OK** if the **Auto** action box comes up.

Using the **Dropper** tool, right-click the purple background to set the background colour to our background colour.

Now with the **Airbrush** tool, right-click to paint over the hole in the canvas, being careful not to paint the other eye.

Subtracting selections

You already know how to add selections by holding down **Shift** as you make a second or third selection. You can also subtract portions of a selection by holding down the **Ctrl** key.

We will paint the mouth using this technique.

Draw a large circle selection from the middle of the eyes.

Now hold the **Ctrl** key down and draw another circle starting from the top of the left-hand eye.

The second circle has eaten away at the first circle, giving us a neat mouth shape.

Figure 3.6: Subtracting selections

Spray the mouth dark purple and, decreasing the opacity to say **10**, spray a small amount of the background colour on the bottom lip.

You will need a good few goes to get a shape you like. It is worth the effort.

Tip:

When you airbrush fine gradients build them up in fine layers and you will get a much better result.

Modifying a selection

Sometimes the selection area is almost, but not quite, what you want. You can modify it.

Note the soft edge to the red mouth.

Click on this cross-hair and you can choose the area on the canvas you want to look at.

- From the **Selection Tool Options** palette select **Modify**. Click **Contract**.
- Set the Contract Selection window to **12** pixels. Press **OK**. You should see the selection has got smaller.
- Go back to the **Selection Tool Options** palette and select **Modify**. This time choose **Feather** and set that to **6** pixels. This will give a soft edge to the selection.
- Colour the selection red and you should have something that looks like figure 3.7.

Figure 3.7: A contracted, feathered selection

- Now select the **Freehand Selection** tool and, holding down the **Ctrl** key, cut out some tombstone teeth like the ones in Figure 3.8.

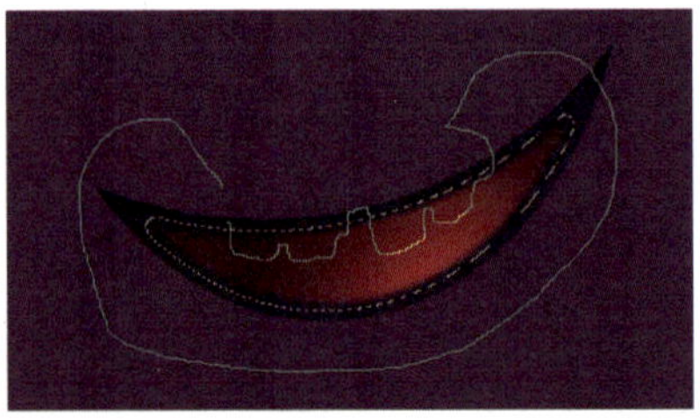

Figure 3.8

- With the **Airbrush** tool, paint the teeth a grimy colour.

- Now using the ellipse **Selection** tool draw the pig's nose. Try to place it slightly over the right eye - you can use the **Move** tool to move the nose to the right place while it is still selected.
- Colour it a lighter purple to match the background.

Look at figure 3.1. Draw and paint the right nostril using a circle or ellipse and carefully spray black around the top of it.

With the nostril selected, select Edit, Copy from the Menu bar.

Now click Edit, Paste, Paste As New Selection. You can drag the nostril to the exact position you want while it is selected simply by moving the cursor. Click when it is in the correct position.

Press Ctrl-D to deselect.

With the Magic Wand selection tool and with the Tolerance set very low, select the purple background.

If you look at Figure 3.1, you will see I have made the pig slightly 3-D on the face by spraying lighter purple above the nose and dark purple under it.

With the airbrush set to Size 250, Hardness 0 and Opacity 15, spray light purple above the nose and dark under it.

Figure 3.9

Now use the Freehand Selection tool to add, in this order, the ears, some manic eyebrows in black and lastly some hair.

The Preset Shape tool

You have learnt a lot about Paint Shop Pro, but there are a lot more fun things hidden away in it.

Using the Preset Shape tool, we will add some mucky food splats to our pig. Set the tool options to match Figure 3.10.

Uncheck **Retain style**, and set the **Width** to **0**.

Set the background colour to a suitable pig-food shade.

From the **Shape list** choose the **Ink Blot** and draw it onto your pig.

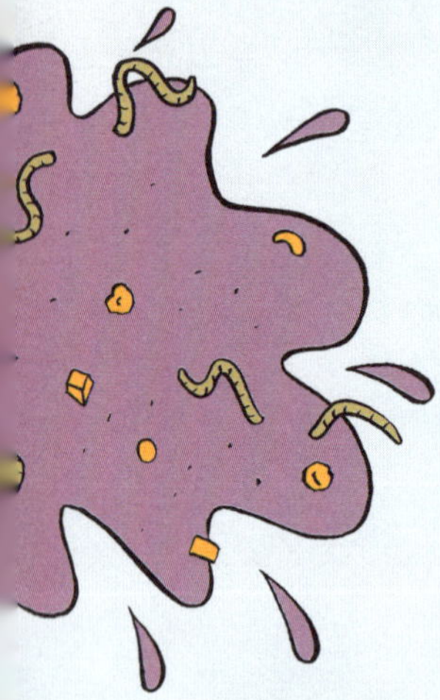

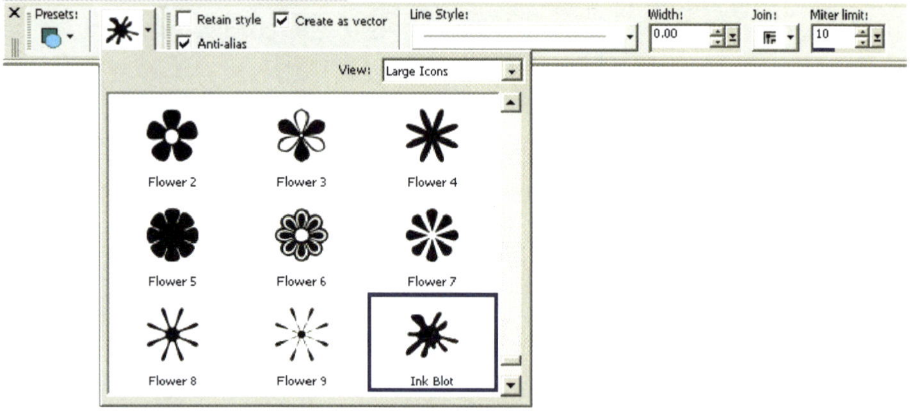

Figure 3.10

Use the nodes around the blot to shape and rotate the object. Remember to press **Ctrl-D** to deselect.

Tip:

Scale the blot up or down by clicking the cursor over these small boxes (nodes) around the shape box. You can move the coloured splat by dragging the centre node.

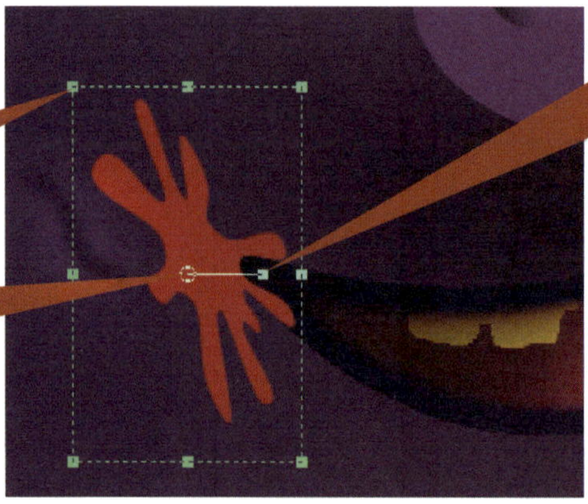

Click the off-centre node to rotate the object

Figure 3.11

Choose a different background colour and add another blot.

Are you pleased with your artwork? Try making a beautiful pig with a flower in her hair!

Tip:

Use the **Object Selector** tool to move the blots if you want to!

Figure 3.12

Chapter 4
Working with Layers

Layers are like transparent sheets arranged on top of each other. They can be arranged in different orders, and switched on and off. You can even make the layers react to different colours or contrasts and blend together to make some spectacular pictures.

Supplied with the Paint Shop Pro program CD are some pictures already in digital form. In the next project we will use one of them.

- Open Paint Shop Pro 8.
- To find an image stored in the computer, from the **File** menu select **Browse**. You'll see a screen similar to Figure 4.1.
- Choose **boat.jpg** by double-clicking its icon. You can close the Browse window now.

If you cannot find the image, it may be downloaded from **www.payne-gallway.co.uk/psp** and stored in a suitable folder.

Figure 4.1: Browsing to find an image

Zoom in and have a look at the picture. We are going to make the boat look like an underwater wreck.

Figure 4.2

We will replace the sand with fallen treasure and seaweed and add a background. We need to think about perspective and how this new scene might look underwater to give it maximum artistic effect.

Selecting an area

First of all we need to delete any evidence of the boat being on land. To do this we need to zoom in on the boat and carefully select only the area around the bow section, excluding the boat from the selection. Here goes.

- Click the **Freehand Selection** tool on the **Tools** toolbar.
- In the **Tool Options** palette set the Selection Type as **Point to point**, set Brush Size to **13** and set Feather to **1**.
- Left-click on the bow, and start drawing along and around the outline of the bow (front) of the boat, including the spar (long horizontal pole).
- When you want to change direction, left-click. When you get back to the first position, **right-click** to close the selection area box. If you make an error, you will need to close the box before you can use **Ctrl-Z** to start again.

Tip:

The **Feather** option slightly blurs the selection line and helps to blend in your retouching. **Antialias** is a digital enhancer that makes the edges on selections and type much neater.

- When you have gone round the bow take the selection down into the sand, up around the buildings and back to the start point. Only the area inside the selection (which now excludes the boat) will be affected by the cloning operation.

Figure 4.3

- Use the **Clone Brush** tool to delete the buildings only. Set the Brush Size to **13**. Try and leave some of the vegetation as in figure 4.3. Remember that to clone an area, you start by right-clicking the area to clone, then 'paint' over the area to be cloned.

- Deselect and choose the **Magic Wand** tool. Set Tolerance to **30** and Feather to **1** pixel. Click on the sandy foreground and select all the sand.

We now have our background and a selection. Now you will learn how easy and useful layers are.

Adding layers

Each update will be added on a separate layer.

- From the **Layers** menu on the Menu bar, select **New Raster Layer**.

- You should now see the New Raster Layer window. Name the layer **Seabed** and click **OK**.

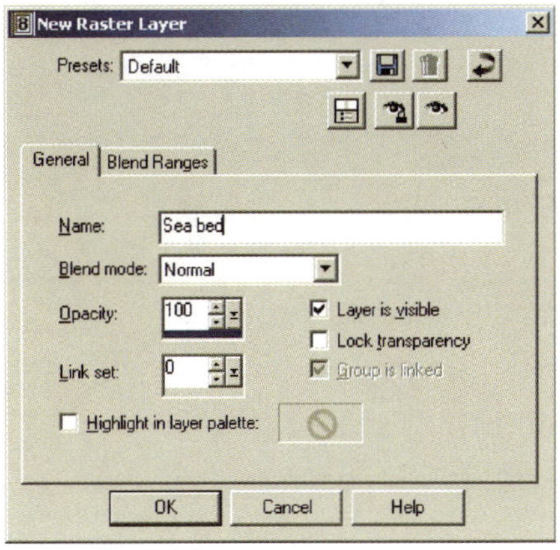

Figure 4.4

Tip:
Another name for **Raster** layer is **Bit-mapped** layer.

Tip:

The function key **F8** is the shortcut key for the **Layers** palette.

In **Auto roll up** mode, the palette automatically 'rolls up' so only the Title bar is visible unless the cursor is over it.

You need to be able to see the Layers palette. If it is not on your screen, from the Menu bar select View, Palettes, Layers. The Layers palette will appear on the left-hand side of the screen.

- Look at the Layers palette. Does it have your new layer called Seabed in it?
- Left-click the Layers palette title bar. A black border will appear and you can now drag the Layers palette over your canvas.
- Your Layers palette is now much easier to see. You can of course drag it back into the Palettes docking section, or by pressing the small arrow in the top right corner you can activate the Auto roll up mode.

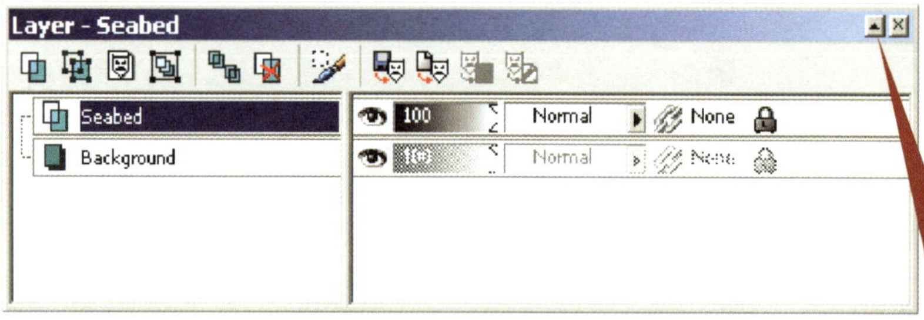

Figure 4.5: The Layers Palette

Lock Window Open/Allow Auto Roll-up

Painting the Seabed

- With the Seabed layer selected, start painting in the selection. Remember that unlike in our atmosphere where everything gets lighter the further away it is, in the sea it is the opposite.
- With Brush Size 50, Hardness 0 and Opacity 10, paint dark blue on the horizon line getting lighter and more yellow the closer the seabed gets.

- Now select the Picture Tube icon and in the library of Tube Options select the Lawn tube.

- As you paint the seaweed lawn, alter the size of the grass from Scale 10 in the distance up to Scale 100 in the foreground. Remember, the further away an object is the smaller it appears.

Figure 4.6

Tip:

Run your cursor over the **Seabed** layer and a small preview window appears.

Press Ctrl-D to deselect all.

Painting rocks and rope

Make a new Raster Layer and call it Rocks and rope.

Again using the Picture Tube icon select River rocks and paint different sized river rocks, getting larger as they get closer to you.

Now choose the picture tube Rope, using only the very smallest size to keep the rope in proportion to the picture. I would suggest 10 far away, 20 middle distance and 30 near.

Make another new layer. This time try using the New Raster Layer icon on the Layers palette.

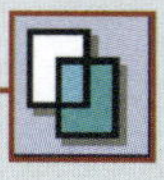

Call the new layer Shadows.

On this new layer, use the Airbrush to spray black shadows under the rocks and rope, trying to make them about the same size as the objects casting them. Remember to change the size of your brush and opacity to say 90.

Tip:

Really concentrate on arranging the rocks - try to make them look convincing. If the Picture Tube brings up a rock that looks wrong, press **Ctrl-Z** and choose another.

Right-click to zoom up, left-click to go back.

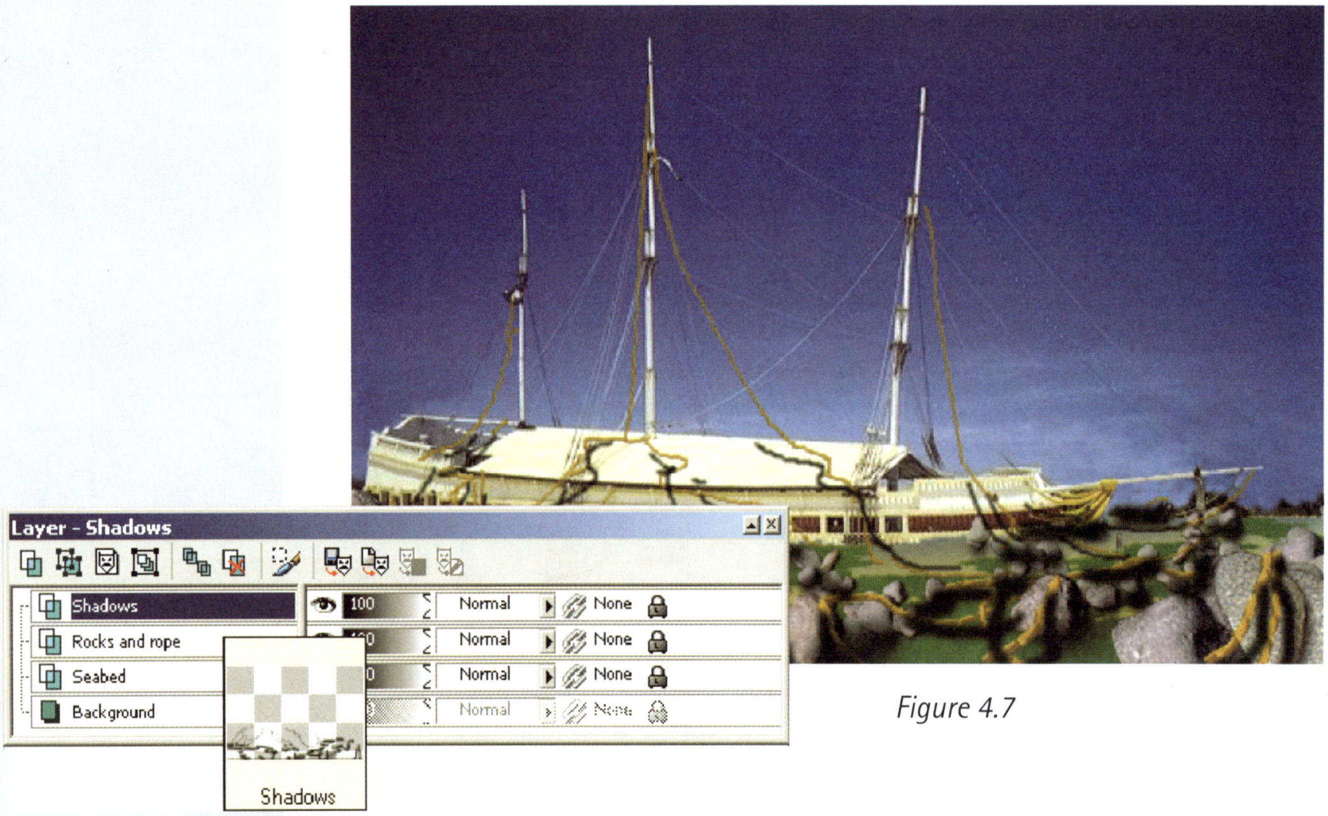

Figure 4.7

The black blobs don't look too much like shadows, but they will once we reshuffle the layers and place the Shadows layer under the Rocks and rope layer.

In the Layers palette click on the Shadows layer and drag it to below the Rocks and rope layer. The layers should now be rearranged.

This is a good time to look at other options in the Layers palette.

Layer options

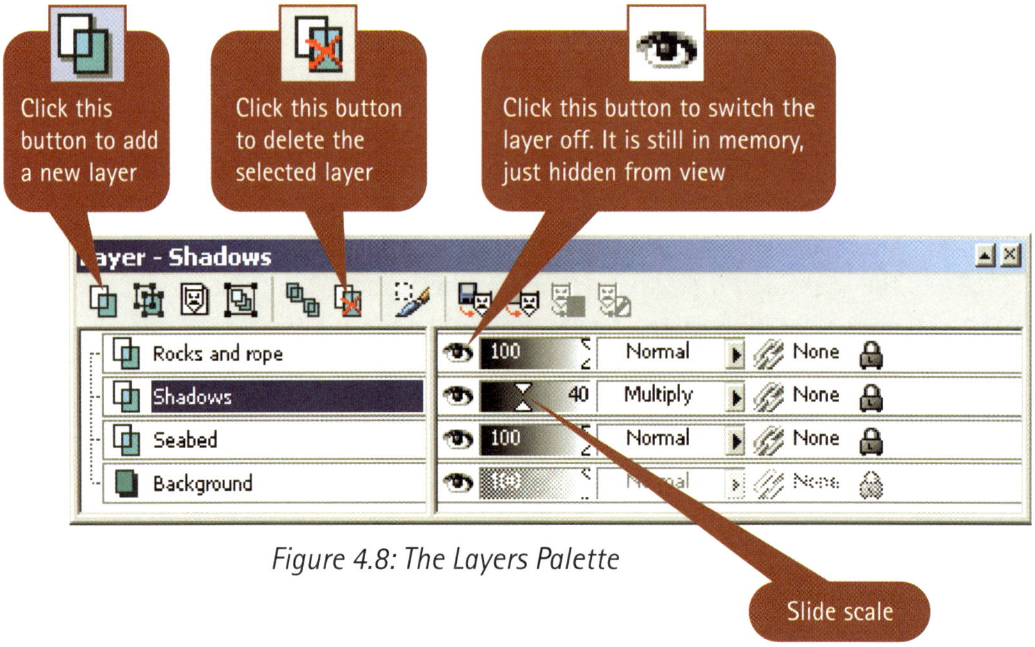

Figure 4.8: The Layers Palette

Try all the different blend settings. The **Multiply** option will darken the seabed layer below your shadow in a realistic manner, but you will need make it less opaque.

On the right-hand side of the **Layers** palette are more options.

In the **Shadow Layer** set the **Blend Mode** to **Multiply** and then using the slide scale, decrease the **Opacity** until the shadows under the **Rocks and rope** layer look realistic.

As an experiment change the slide scale of the rocks and rope layer – see how it becomes quite ghostly.

If your shadows need tweaking a bit you can spray more on or use the **Eraser** tool to refine the shape.

Figure 4.9

Tip:

Remember to try to match the darkness of your shadows with your existing shadows. Also note the direction of the shadows in the picture and try to replicate this.

Select the **Shadows** layer and spray your shadow colour to refine the shadows. Note how your **Airbrush** sprays in the blended mode!

Use the **Eraser** tool as well.

Switch the layers on and off to see what a difference you have made.

Change the **Blend Modes** in the **Rocks and rope** layer – the effects are wild. OK, now set it back to **Normal**. I hope it's giving you ideas for your next piece of art.

Painting the sea

This will be fun. Make a New Raster Layer and call it Sea. Now select the Airbrush and paint a canvas like Figure 4.10, trying to match the colours. Use a large, soft brush and medium opacity.

Minimise, Maximise and **Close.**

Click the Maximise icon to give yourself some space around the picture. This makes it easier to spray the sky from edge to edge.

Make sure it is at the top of the layer stack.

Figure 4.10

Tip:

If it seems too dark, drag the layers slide to **90%**.

Now change the layer blend mode to Multiply. How do you like that? Try some other blend modes; some of the effects are quite surprising.

Now, make a new layer called Ripples and light. Using white and various Airbrush sizes (but never more than 30), Hardness 0, and Opacity 2, paint ripples in the water. Make the ripples thinner and closer together as they go into the distance.

Change the Blend option to Overlay. Use Figure 4.11 as reference.

Now painting in the overlay blend mode paint some more ripples including some on the seabed – it looks like the light reflecting on the bottom.

Choose the Dry brush from the Brush Shapes menu and using Opacity 50, paint shafts of light through the seawater. After you have finished, choose Default (the first option) from the Brush Shapes menu.

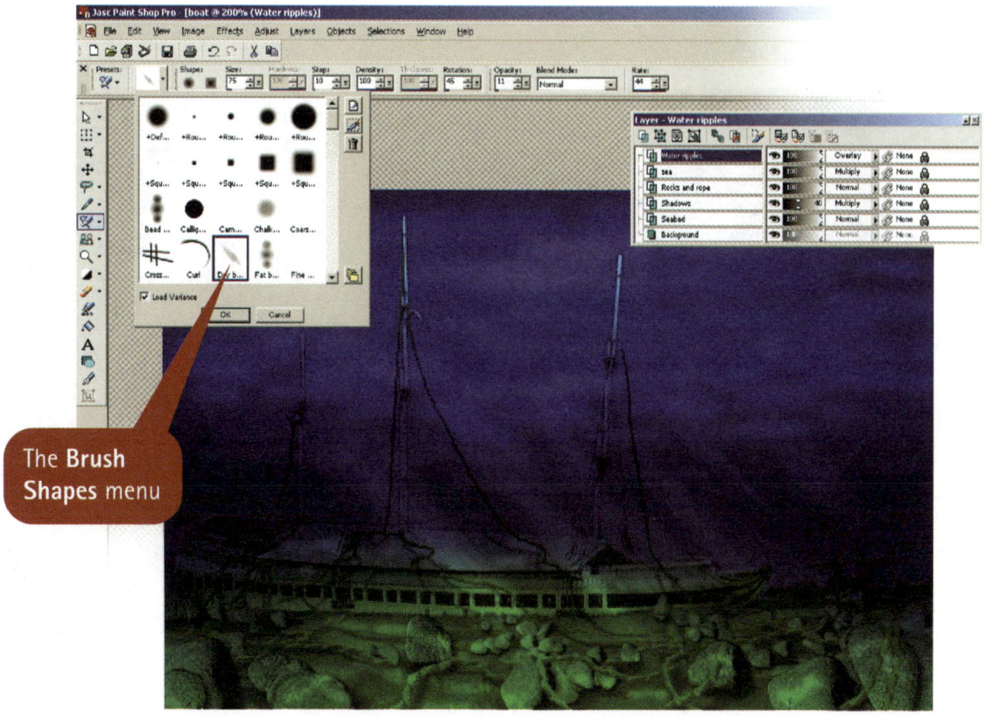

Figure 4.11

Make a new layer called **Cave**. Make sure the **Cave** layer is selected and is on the top of the layer pile.

Use the **Freehand Selection** tool to draw a cave mouth round the edge of the picture, and then paint the selection black. The **Selection Type** should be **Freehand**. If you have only selected the inside of the cave you may have to **Invert** in the **Selections** menu to be able to paint your cave black.

Deselect.

Now choose the **Picture Tube**, select the **Vine leafy** tube, Scale **50** and paint a little bit around the cave entrance, then add a little **Rope** size **100**. Remember, less is more! Have a look at what I did in Figure 4.12.

Now as a preview to the next section go to the Menu bar and choose **Adjust**, **Brightness and Contrast**, **Brightness/Contrast**.

In the Brightness/Contrast window, change Brightness to **–150** and leave Contrast at **50**. Click **OK**.

It should have gone quite dark; now go to **Adjust** again but choose **Blur** and **Blur more**.

That has given a lot of depth to our picture. All there is left to do is to add some bubbles using white and a **Paint Brush** set at Size **2** and Opacity **50**.

Tip:

Don't forget if you are not happy, throw the layer away, get yourself a new one and have another go.

Tip:

Try switching all the layers off to see just what a difference you have made.

OK, that should do it. Your first major photo retouching is complete and it shows how useful layers are.

Figure 4.11

Now you can save your image. Be sure and save it as a Paint Shop Pro Image **(.pspimage)** file. If you try to save it as, for example, a **.jpg** file you may see a message:

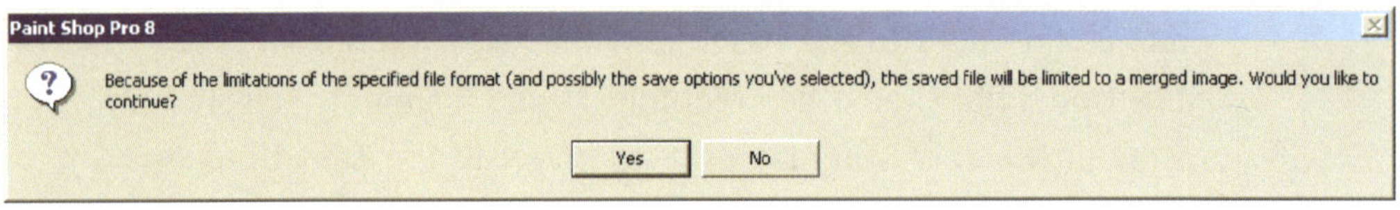

Figure 4.12

If you click **Yes**, you will lose the layers that you used to create your picture.

Well done, print out to show off your artwork.

Chapter 5
Effects

By adding different effects to a picture you can create some spectacular results very quickly. In this project you will turn a white canvas into an African savannah with the help of your artistic eye and some special effects.

Experimenting with effects

- Open Paint Shop Pro.
- Open a new canvas, and make it 800 pixels wide, 500 high, with a white background.
- Paint a background like Figure 5.1. From the Menu bar select Adjust, Blur, Gaussian blur set to 18 and click OK.
- Now paint some clouds, using the Airbrush tool loaded with white. Use a darker blue background colour to paint shadows under the clouds.

Figure 5.1

Changing the hue

One of my favourite effects is the negative filter. It makes everything invert so that white becomes black and so on. In our case it will help turn daylight into sunset.

- On the Menu bar choose **Adjust**, **Negative Image**.
- Now select **Adjust**, **Hue & Saturation**, **Hue/Saturation/Lightness**.

We need to give an orange hue to the picture.

- Make sure the **Colorize** box is ticked. Move the **Hue** handle until you have an orange shade. Then move the **Saturation** handle up to brighten the colour.

You can see the effect in the right-hand picture in the Hue/Saturation/Lightness window. The settings should be approximately as shown in Figure 5.2.

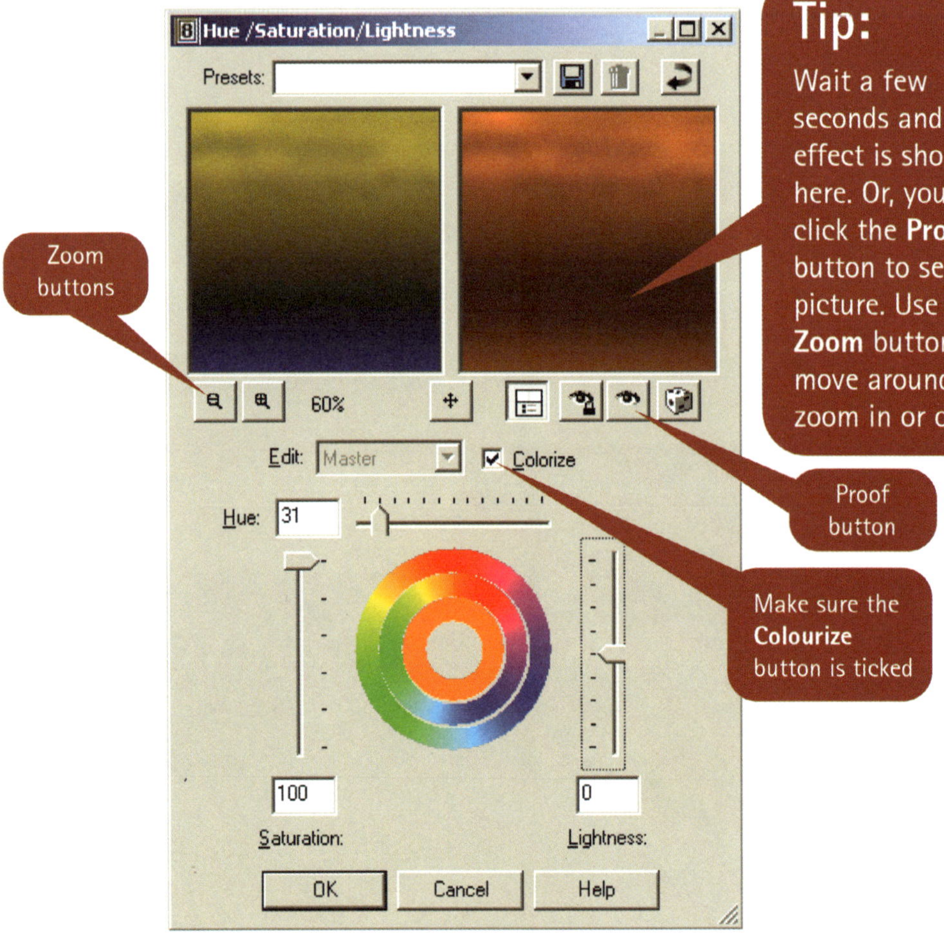

Figure 5.2: Changing Hue, Saturation and Lightness

Tip:

Wait a few seconds and the effect is shown here. Or, you can click the **Proof** button to see your picture. Use the **Zoom** buttons to move around and zoom in or out.

- Make a new Raster layer and call it **Savanna**. From the **Tools** toolbar click the **Selection** tool and draw a rectangular selection from the bottom corner up to your horizon line. Fill it with black and then deselect.
- Using the picture tube **Grass blades**, paint grass over the black box. Use between **10** and **20** on the Scale option and make sure you completely cover the black rectangle.
- Now select **Adjust**, **Hue & Saturation**, **Hue/Saturation/Lightness**. Set the lightness to **–100** and click **OK**.
- Select **Background** in the **Layers** palette, and spray a blue line across the horizon using a large soft Airbrush and opacity of **2**, to build it up gently.
- Make a new Raster layer called **Wild life** and position it below the **Savanna** layer. Now choose an animal or two from the **Picture Tube**, **Zoo Animal**. Paint them in your scene.
- Click the **Deform Tool** on the **Tools** toolbar, and adjust the scale/position and orientation of your chosen animals.

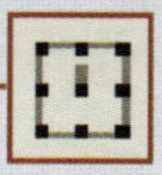

Tip:
If you need to spray/paint a straight line, click the start point, press and hold the **Shift** key and click the end point, hey presto.

Make sure in the **Deform** Tool option that **Scale X%** and **Scale Y%** are the same values or you might get some very long or squat animals.

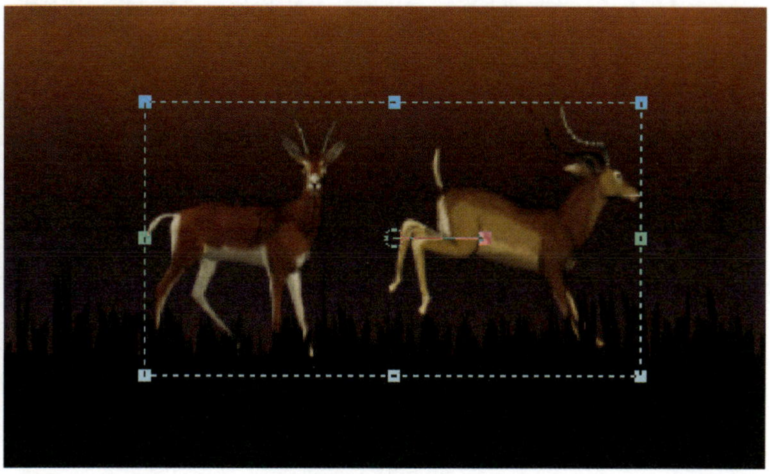

Figure 5.3

Zooming in

You can zoom in on a portion of the picture using the **Zoom** tool.

- To deselect the **Deform** tool you will need to click another tool.
- Click the **Zoom** tool and click on an animal face. Keep clicking, zooming in closer and closer.

At some point you will see that the image is made up of different coloured squares, called pixels.

Figure 5.4: A close-up view of the pixels, which make up the picture

Tip:

The image size is displayed in the bottom right-hand corner of the screen.

When you zoom in, the pixels are shown larger. The more pixels per inch, the higher the resolution.

This image is 800 pixels wide and 500 high, and the image cannot be viewed any bigger at the set resolution because there is no more information stored. It is a bitmap or raster image.

There is another type of image called a vector image that can be scaled or viewed at any size and you will never see any pixels. You will work with vector images in the next chapter.

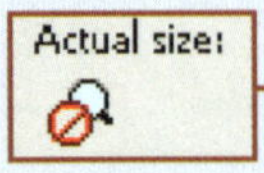

- Click the Normal Viewing button to return to Normal view.

Adding trees and mountains

- From the Layers menu select New Raster Layer to make a new layer called Trees. Leave the default options and click OK.
- With the Freehand Selection tool set to Freehand in the Tool Options palette, draw some trees silhouette style. (Look at figure 5.7 for reference.) Colour them blue; spray them lightly so some background colour comes through.
- From the Menu bar select Adjust, Blur, Motion Blur, and set Angle to 90, Strength to 15%.
- Now do the same again with a new layer but draw some hills and a mountain in the background.
- To make the mountain appear farther away, choose Adjust, Blur, Blur More.

Make sure your layers are in this order:

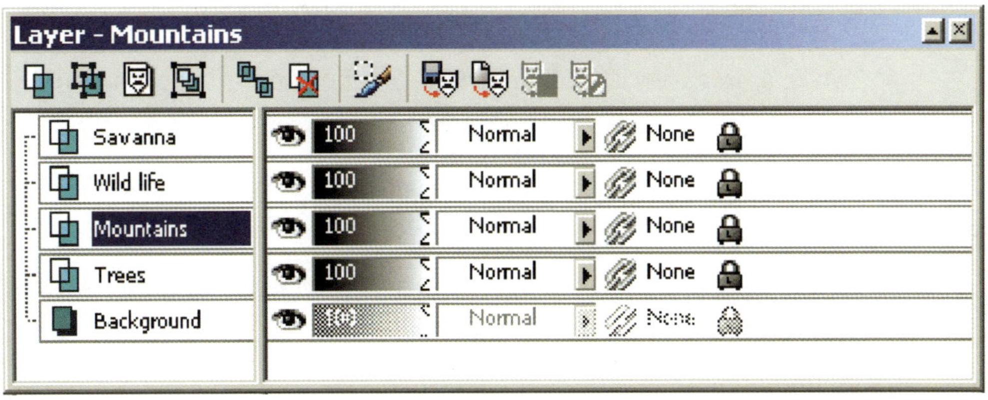

Figure 5.5

Select the Background layer.

From the Effects menu on the Menu bar select Illumination Effects, Sunburst. You will see a window like Figure 5.6.

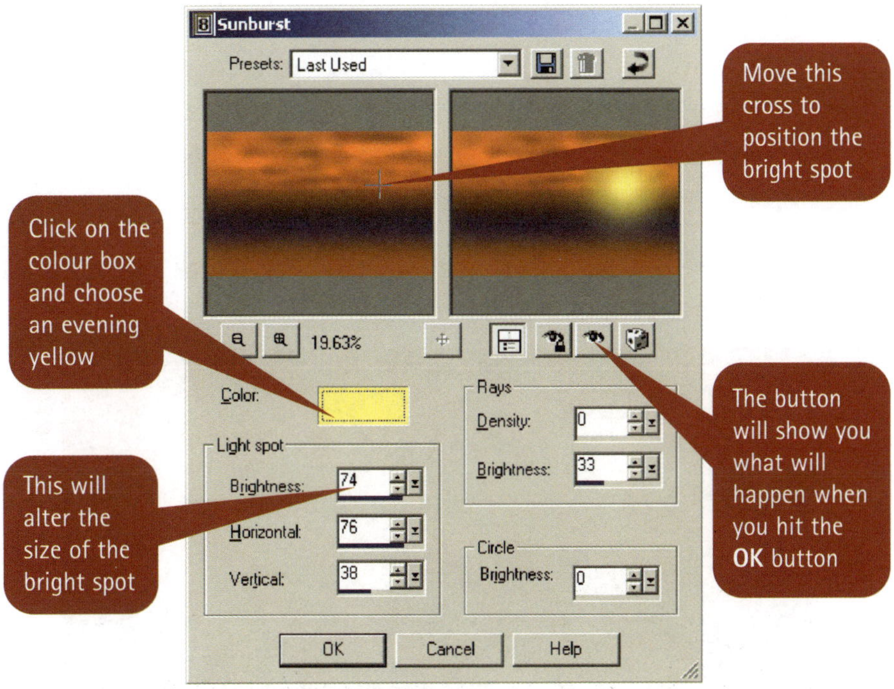

Figure 5.6

Applying effects in selections

Select the Wild life layer. Choose an animal and using the Freehand Selection tool draw around the animal, making sure there is space around it.

To give it a bit of movement click Adjust, Blur, Motion Blur, Angle to 90 degrees and Strength to 10%.

Adding a lightning strike

- Make a new layer called Lightning, and position it under the Wild life layer.
- Select the Picture Tube and find Lightning.
- Position a lightning strike on to your picture; make sure the strike is big enough to cross the sky area.
- Use the Mover tool to adjust the position of the strike.
- From the Adjust menu select Blur, Motion Blur. Try the effect of setting the Angle and Strength, to give the lightning some movement.
- Change the Lightning layer blend mode to Screen. Looks fantastic, doesn't it.
- Lastly, move the slide scale in the Layers palette to make the mountains lighter than the trees and the trees lighter than the foreground.
- Now save your picture and make sure you save it as a Paintshop Pro Image (.psp or .pspimage).

Figure 5.7

Merging layers

You can merge all the layers and then try some global effects. Don't overwrite the layered version you have already saved though – you may need it again!

- From the Layers menu select Merge, Merge All (Flatten).

Other effects

Try out some other effects. Here are some suggestions:

From the **Effects** menu select **Distortion Effects**, **Spiky Halo** and try various settings. (This effect concentrates your eye on the centre of the picture.)

(You can either click **OK** or **Cancel**, then go on to the next one. Save any that you like as a new file.)

From the **Effects** menu select **Image Effects**, **Seamless Tiling**. (This one is great for creating posters or a background for a web site.)

The last effect I wanted to try is one that looks like a painting.

I loaded up my saved **Paint Shop Pro** layered file and switched the **Lightning Layer** off. Don't forget to then click **Layers**, **Merge**, **Merge All (Flatten)** so that you can apply a global effect.

Select **Effects**, **Art Media Effects**, **Brush Strokes** and experiment with different settings. You should end up with something that looks like an oil painting!

Here is a portfolio of my finished pictures.

Chapter 6

Vector Graphics

Raster or bitmap images are made up from an array of different coloured pixels. The resolution of a picture is measured typically in pixels per inch (ppi) or dots per inch (dpi), and the more pixels per inch, the finer the detail in the picture. Raster images are very good for storing and changing photographic style pictures but if you enlarge the image, the results will probably not be satisfactory and individual pixels will be visible.

Vector images are made from mathematical information about the curves, sizes, and point positions and colours. Whenever you change the size of a vector image, rotate it or skew the image, it is redrawn and will be perfect. This type of image is good for graphical shapes or text. We are now going to create a vector image.

The Yellow Submarine

Open a new canvas 600 pixels wide and 400 high. Specify Vector Background, and click OK.

Make the foreground colour black by clicking black in the Materials palette. Set the background to Transparent.

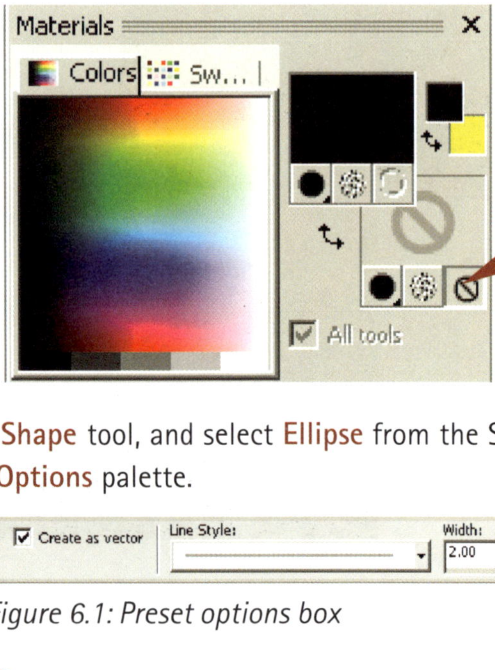

The background style is set to **transparent** so that the ellipse will not be filled with the background colour automatically.

Click the Preset Shape tool, and select Ellipse from the Shape list box in the Tool Options palette.

Figure 6.1: Preset options box

Draw the first ellipse for the submarine's body as in Figure 6.2. You can move it by dragging the centre node, and size it by dragging a node on the box surrounding it. Then draw the second smaller one. Remember to deselect after each part is drawn.

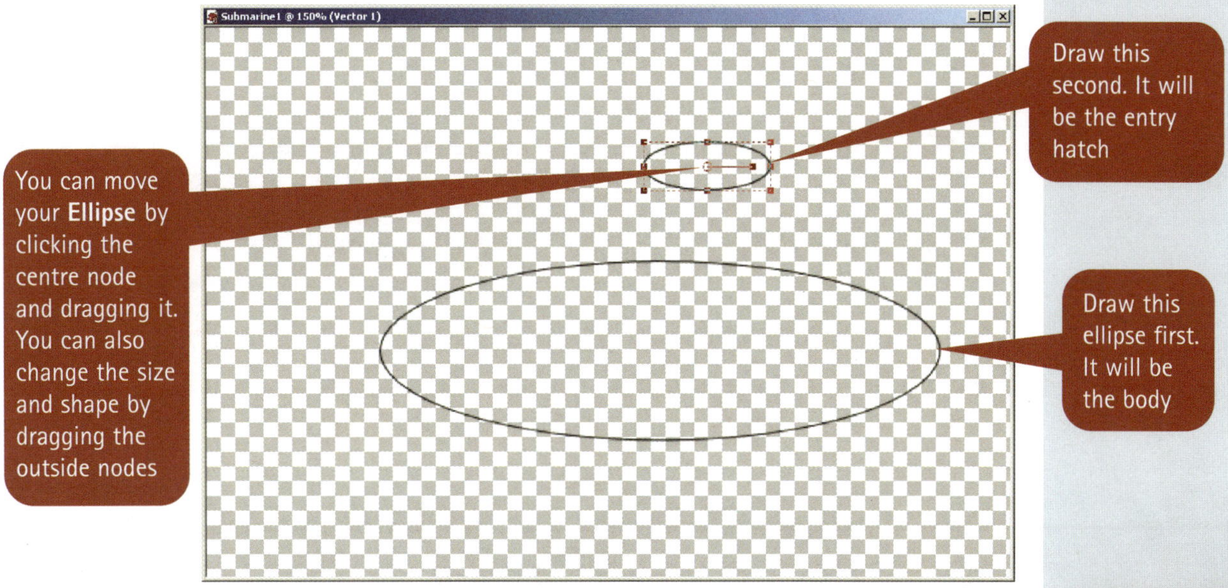

Figure 6.2

Select the **Rounded Rectangle** in the Shape list options and follow the order shown in Figure 6.3.

Note:

You will see the reason for drawing them in order when you colour the shapes.

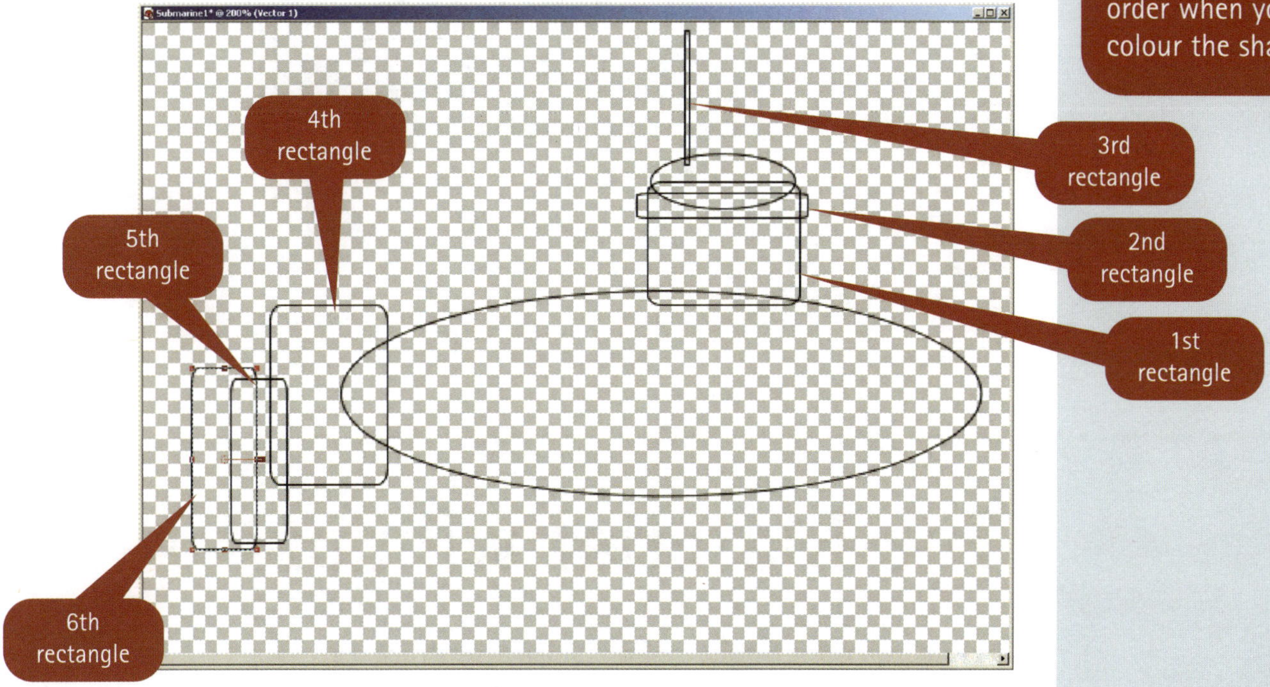

Figure 6.3

Don't worry if the shape and size look a bit out – you can adjust anything later.

Selecting a Fill colour and style

Right, let's colour our submarine.

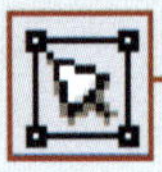

- Start by selecting the submarine body using the **Object Selection** tool.
- On the Menu bar, choose **Objects**, **Properties**.

The Vector Properties box opens as in Figure 6.4. The **Stroke** refers to the outline of an object. You can 'stroke' using brushes of different widths, line styles, textures and colours.

The **Fill** can also be in different patterns, textures and colours. We are going to fill with a solid colour.

Tip:

You can also right-click on the Canvas, and choose **Properties**.

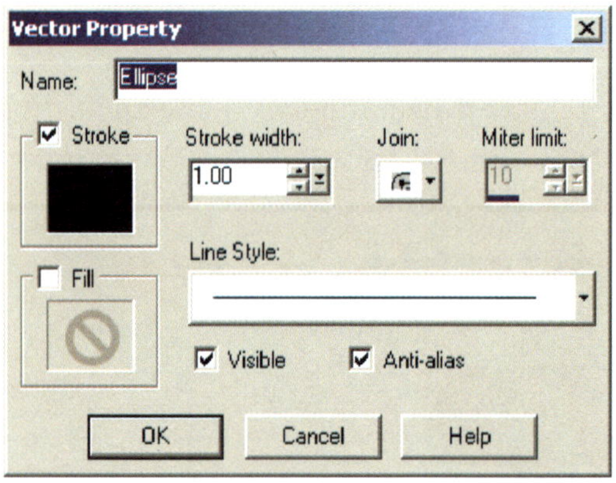

Figure 6.4

- Set the Stroke width to **2**.
- Click the Stroke color box.

The Material window

The **Material** window opens. With the **Color** tab selected you can select a colour from the basic palette of 16 colours, or you can move the little circles either in the square on the right or its surrounding circle to pick a more subtle colour.

Every colour is made up of a combination of red, green and blue. You can also type in values between 0 and 255 for red, green and blue, and values for hue, saturation and light.

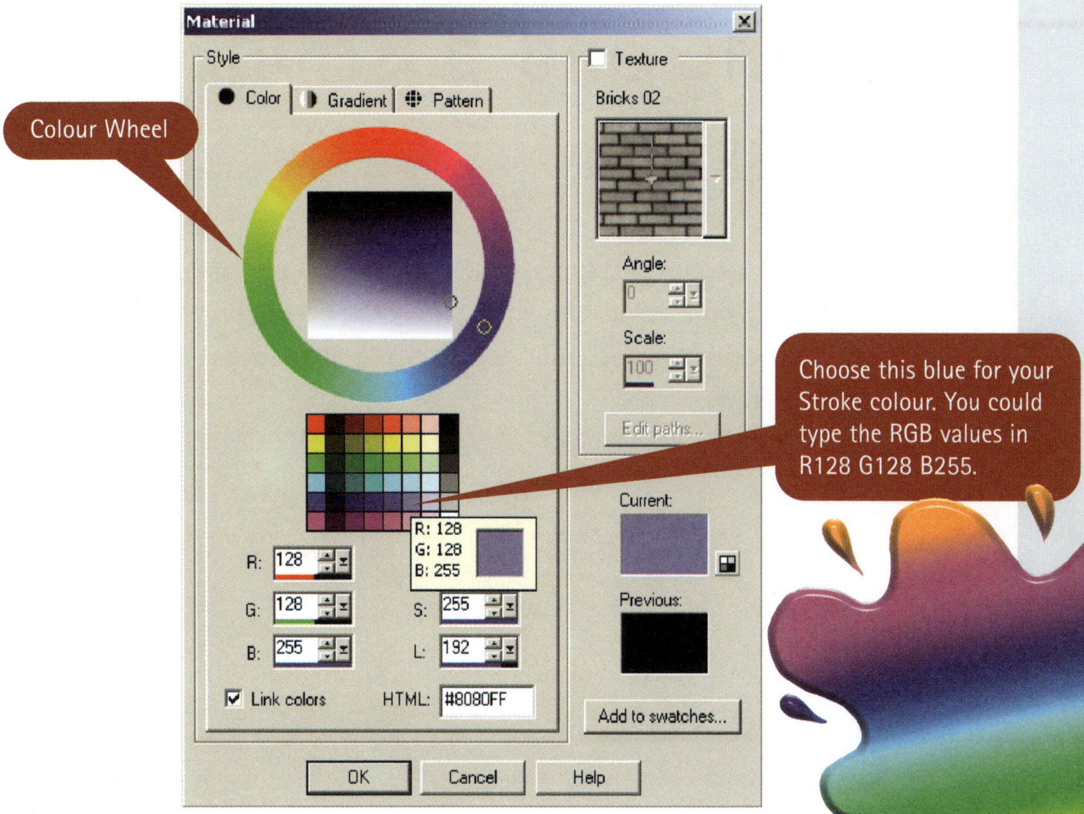

Figure 6.5 Material window

- Click the blue colour shown in Figure 6.5 and click **OK**.
- Select the **Fill** box and then click in the **Fill Color** box again to choose bright yellow (R255/G255/B000).

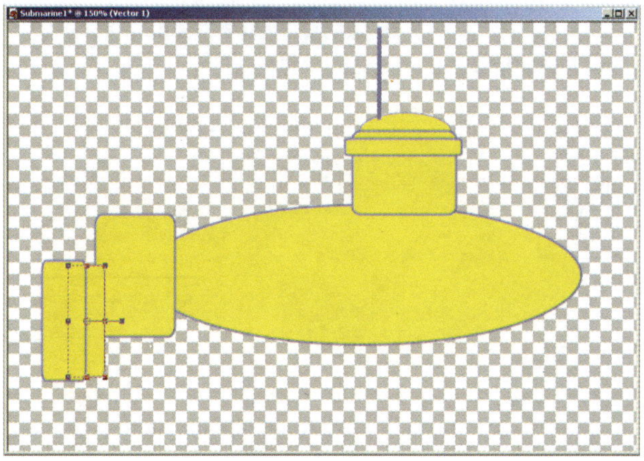

Figure 6.6

- Go through all your shapes and colour them as above. (You can select more than one by holding down **Shift** as you select.).
- Select the shape that I have selected in Figure 6.6.
- Right-click and choose **Arrange**, **Send To Bottom**.
- Now right-click, select **Properties**, and using the colour wheel make the yellow fill slightly darker.

Tip:

If a shape is in the wrong order you can move it up or down by selecting it with the **Object Selection** tool, right-clicking the canvas and choosing **Arrange** to **move up** or **move down**. Or, select **Objects**, **Arrange** on the **Menu** bar.

Copying and pasting objects

We need some port holes so select the **Preset Shapes** tool, **Ellipse**, and draw one under the entry hatch. Deselect and using the **Object Selection** tool select your porthole. You can move it to position it accurately.

Figure 6.7

Tip:

By holding down **Shift** when you draw the ellipse you will draw a perfect circle.

Right-click and choose **Properties**. This time we will choose **Gradient** in the **Fill colour** section.

Match the settings in Figure 6.8. Click **OK**, and **OK** again in the Vector Property window.

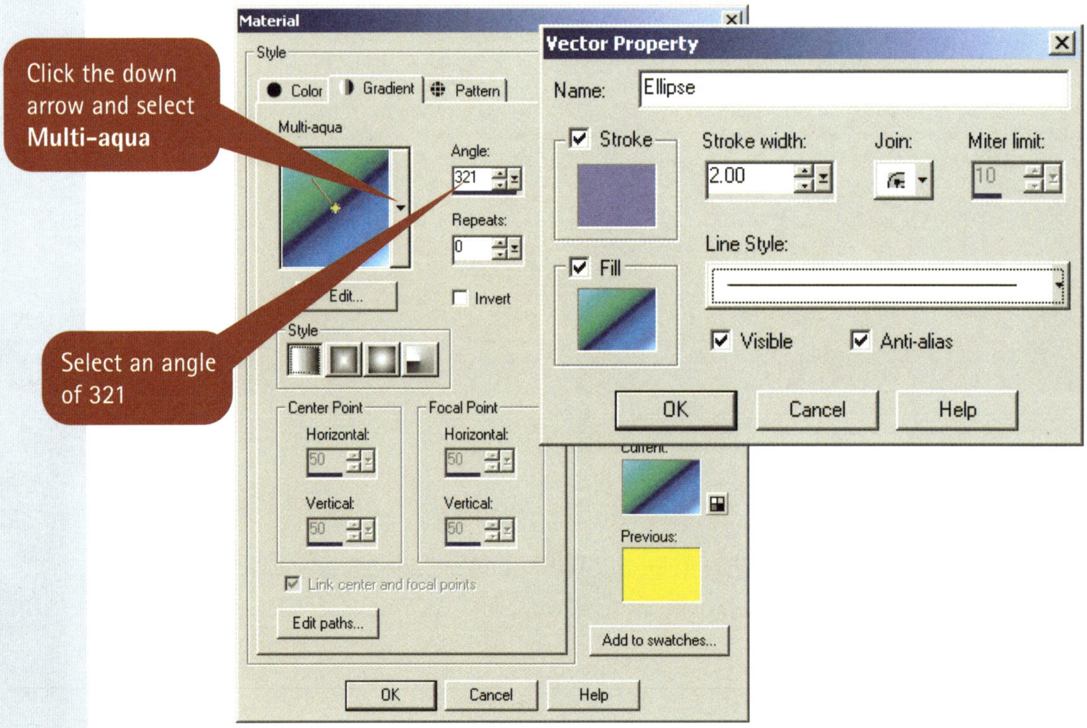

Figure 6.8: Gradient and properties

With the circle selected, right-click and select **Copy**.

Right-click again and click **Paste New Vector Selection**. Move it to the right of the porthole and click.

Squash the circle into an ellipse.

Right-click the new porthole, copy and select **Paste New Vector Selection** on the other side of the circle.

Figure 6.9 portholes!

The Pen tool

You will find there is a limit to what you can achieve with the **Preset Shape Tool**. With the **Pen tool** you will be able to create and manipulate custom shapes.

You can also manipulate the preset shapes by dragging individual nodes and groups of nodes.

With the **Object Selection** tool, select the rudder on the submarine.

Now click the **Pen Tool**, and notice the nodes on the rudder have changed. Try dragging them to make the shape in Figure 6.10.

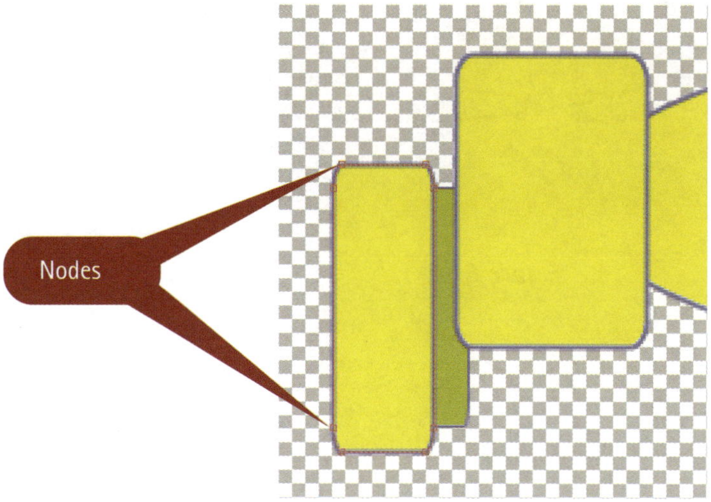

Figure 6.10

Tip:

You can select multiple nodes by holding down **Shift** as you click each one.

Now we will add some lines of rivets to the submarine body.

- With the **Pen** tool still selected, right-click and select **New Drawing object**.
- In the **Pen Options** palette, set the **Line Style** to **Dot** and the **Width** to **2.00**.

The **Tool Options** palette should have settings as shown in Figure 6.11.

Figure 6.11

The Pen tool will draw objects in the current foreground colour so select a suitable colour.

- Click (and release) where you want a line of rivets to start. Then click again where you want the line to end.
- If the line is not quite straight, you can drag either of the end nodes.
- Select **New Drawing Object** before drawing the next line of rivets. (If you forget, simply click the **Undo** button and try again.)

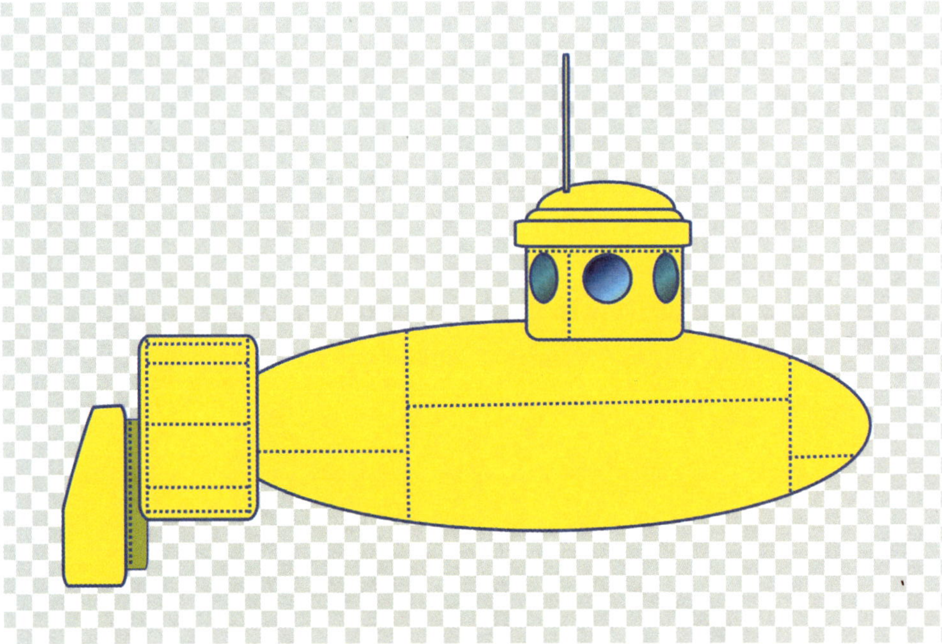

Figure 6.12

Draw a square over the entire canvas and fill it with a dark blue.

Right-click the canvas and select **Arrange**, **Send To Bottom**.

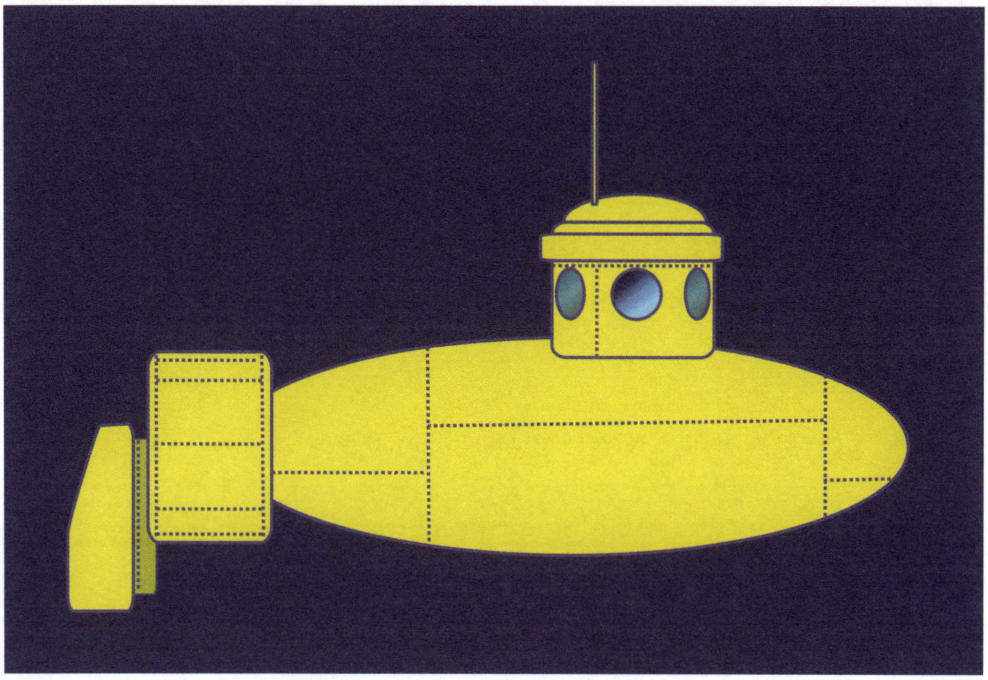

Figure 6.13: The finished graphic

Deselect, save and print out your first vector picture!

Finally, check the size in bytes of this image compared with previous images you have saved. You will find that this is much smaller – another advantage of vector graphics!

We have only touched on the capabilities of the **Pen** tool in this chapter. Drawing curves and using **control arms** is beyond the scope of this book but you may want to experiment on your own.

Chapter **7**

Text Effects

Let's look at some funky text projects. Your first project will be to create a button with some text that you could use on a web site.

- Open a new blue raster canvas 400 by 80 pixels.

The text that you write will be in the current background colour, and it will automatically appear in a new Vector layer named **Vector 1**.

- Change the background colour to a deep yellow.
- Click the **Text** tool. In the **Tool Options** palette select **Create as Vector**. Select a font that you like the look of – the one shown below is **Lucida Handwriting Italic**, size **36**.

Figure 7.1: The Text Tool Options palette

- Click on the canvas and type **Click to enter** in the Text Entry box.

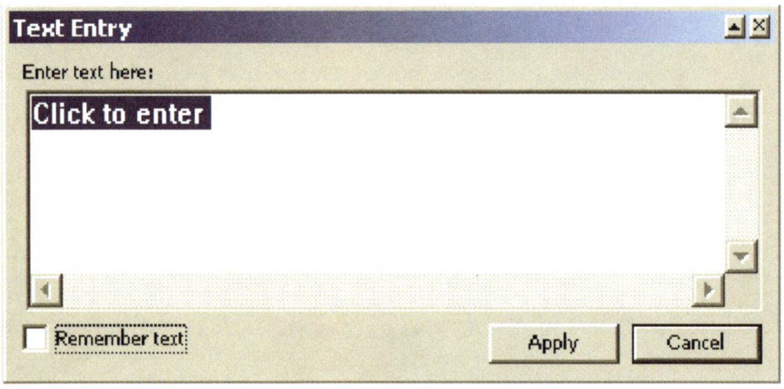

Figure 7.2: Entering text

- Click **Apply**. Position your text using the centre node and size it using the outside nodes.

Figure 7.3

In the **Layers Palette**, right-click the **Vector 1** layer and select **Convert to Raster Layer**. (You cannot apply effects to a Vector layer.)

Right-click again and select **Rename**. Name the layer **Words**.

From the **Effects** menu select **3D Effects**, **Drop Shadow**. Use the settings in Figure 7.4, and click **OK**.

In the **Layers** palette select the **Background** layer and from the **Effects** menu select **3D Effects**, **Inner Bevel**.

Use Figure 7.5 to create the bevel effect.

Tip:

You will see a message telling you that 'The target must be promoted to a full layer'. Just click **OK**.

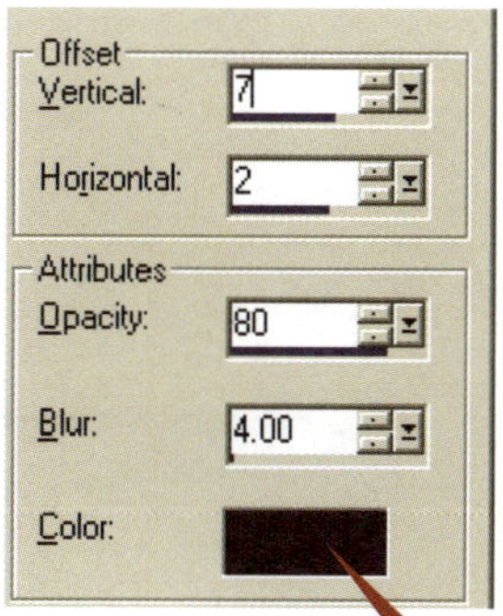

Figure 7.4

Use black or a very dark blue

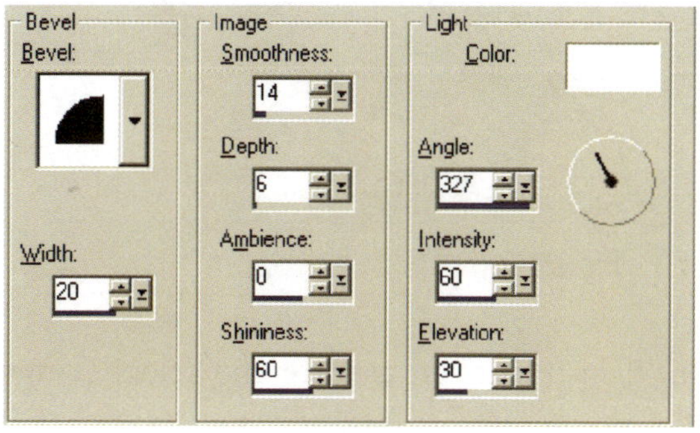

Figure 7.5

You can use the **Mover** tool to shift the text layer so it sits perfectly in your button.

You should end up with a button like the one shown below. You could use something similar on a web site.

Figure 7.6

Using multiple effects

This time we will use multiple effects (filters) to get great results.

- Open a new **Transparent** raster canvas **800** x **200** pixels.
- Make the background colour steel grey.
- Set the options as shown in Figure 7.7, with bold, underlined text.
- Using the **Text** icon write the word **Chrome**.

Make the **Background** box a steel grey colour. The font is Copperplate Gothic Bold size 72

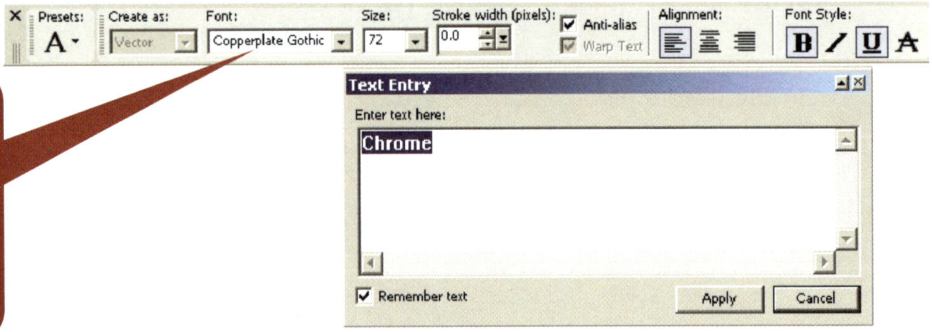

Figure 7.7

- Size the text using the nodes so it is nice and big.

Figure 7.8

- Right-click layer **Vector 1** in the **Layers** palette and select **Convert to Raster layer**. Right-click again and rename this layer **Text**.
- From the **Effects** menu select **Texture Effects**, **Sculpture**. Set the Pattern to **Silver** and use the settings shown below.

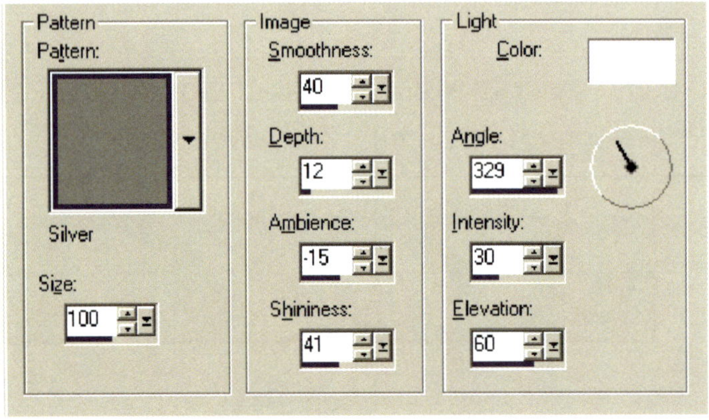

Figure 7.9

From the **Effects** menu select **Artistic effect**, **Chrome**. Use the settings shown in Figure 7.10 (Flaws **4**, Brightness **60**, **Use Original color**) and then click **OK**.

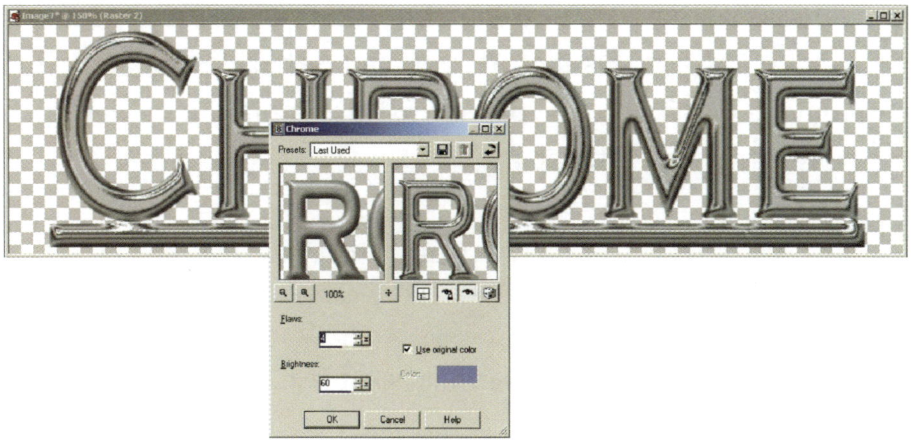

Figure 7.10

Click the background layer **Raster 1** in the **Layers** palette. Using the **Airbrush**, colour it bright blue.

From the **Effects** menu select **Illumination Effects**, **Sunburst**. Use the cross to place the sunburst behind the top of the **H**. You won't be able to see the effect until you click the **Proof** button. Keep clicking the **Proof** button and moving the cross till you are satisfied.

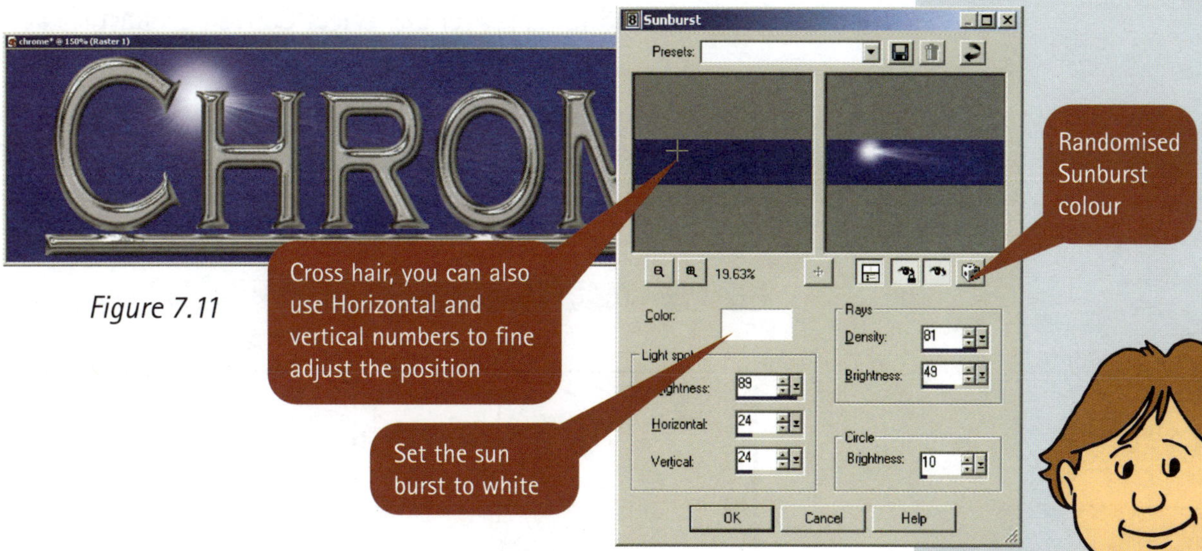

Figure 7.11

Finally on **Layer 1** in the **Layers** palette, using the **Airbrush**, spray a little white highlight over the top edge of the character nearest to the sunburst.

Save your masterpiece!

Figure 7.12

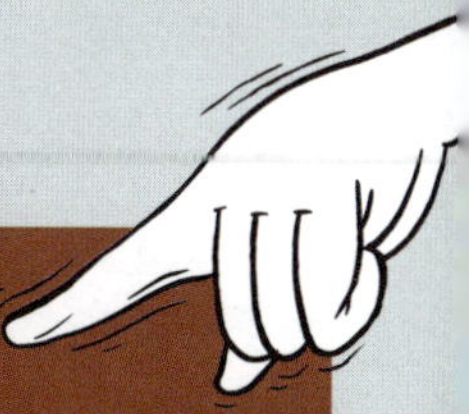

Note:

Copy my settings carefully to get the best result, and experiment to see what happens if you deselect **Use original colour**. Remember you can see the effect of changes by clicking the **Proof** button in the **Chrome** window.

Tip:

Set the opacity of the Airbrush to about **20** and the size to about **35**. You could also spray some extra highlights on a few other letters to give it some real zing.

Creating a poster

We will make a poster using a picture that you created earlier. If you have not got this picture, you can either download it from www.payne-gallway.co.uk/psp or just use a plain blue background to practise the text effects.

- Open the file Shipwreck.pspimage that you created in Chapter 4, or if you have not got it, a new raster canvas in a deep blue colour.
- Make a New Vector Layer, and call it Text.
- Make your background colour bright yellow.
- Select the Type tool and in the Tool Options palette, select Font Snap ITC, size 48. Click on the canvas and type Ship Wreck.
- Position and size your text using the centre and outside nodes.
- Check that your Text layer is on the top in the Layers palette, then right-click the Text layer and select Convert to Raster Layer.

We now can use any of our effects on the Text layer.

- Select Effects, Distortion Effects, Ripple. Use the settings shown below.

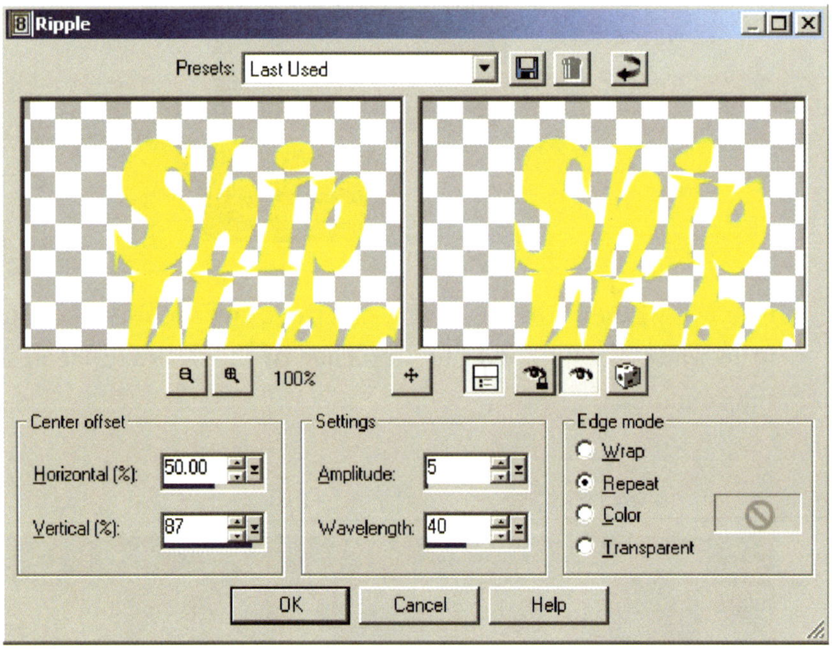

Figure 7.14

Now use **Effects**, **Distortion Effect**, **Wave**. These two effects give a really great feeling of text being refracted by water.

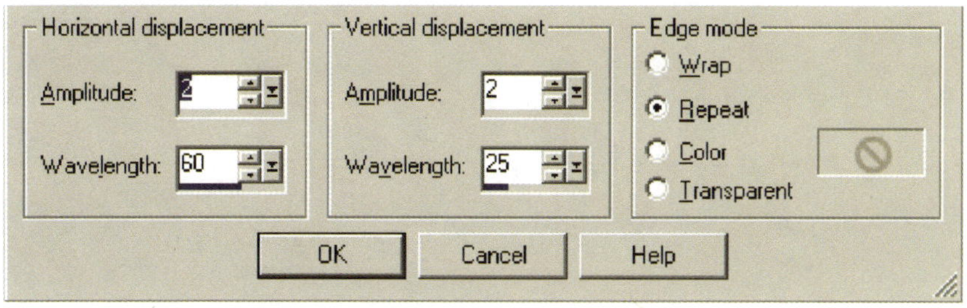

Figure 7.15: Settings for Wave Distortion effect

Hit **OK** and finish off the next blockbuster movie poster with **Effects**, **3D Effects**, **Drop Shadow**. Experiment with the settings and click **OK** when you are happy.

Now create your own masterpiece!

Figure 7.16 Finished poster artwork.

The warp effect makes the text look more like it is underwater.

Chapter 8
Optimising Images

Removing red eye

First of all we are going to look at ways of touching up a photograph that you might, for example, want to post on a web site or e-mail to a friend.

You will need the Paint Shop Pro CD, or you can download the image from www.payne-gallway.co.uk/psp.

Open Paint Shop Pro and from the File menu select Browse. Click the CD icon and then Sample Images. Select RedEye.jpg by double-clicking the icon.

You will notice that the children have red eye, a common problem in photography. We will fix it and optimise the picture as a .jpg for the web.

From the Adjust menu select Red-eye Removal.

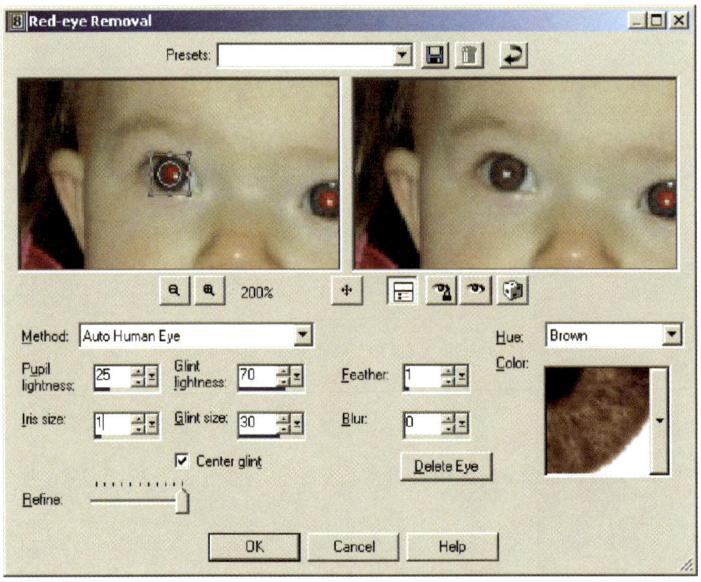

Figure 8.1

Look in the *right* Red-eye Removal frame. With the hand icon, move the picture so you have an eye centred in the window. Zoom in to get a good look at the eye.

You will get a cross hair in the *left* Red-eye Removal frame. Aim it at the centre of the eye and click, holding the mouse button down; draw out until the iris is selected. Finally adjust by using the nodes.

Try the settings as in Figure 8.2. Keep checking with the Proof button till you are satisfied, then click OK.

Now redo the process for the other eye and the next child - don't forget to change the eye colour.

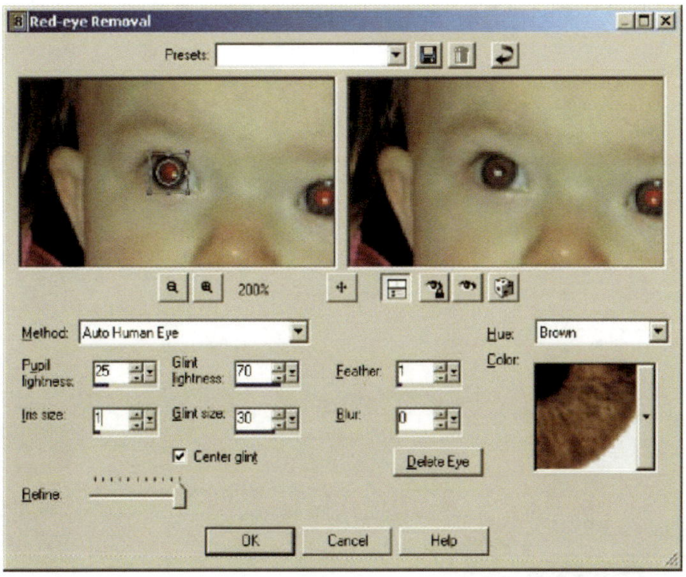

Figure 8.2

Let's frame our corrected kids. On the Menu bar, select Image, Picture frame. I chose Wood Matte. Check Frame outside of the image and click OK.

Go to Layers, Merge, Merge All(Flatten).

Save your picture for the next exercise.

Figure 8.3: Finished picture

Keep adjusting the second eye, as it is easy to make your subject look cross-eyed.

Tip:

Remember you can use the Clone Brush to touch up your photos if you scan them into your computer. (Look back to Chapter 3 if you can't remember how to use the Clone Brush.)

Optimising for the Web

When you save images to go onto the World Wide Web you need to make sure the file sizes are as small as possible to keep the download times short.

There are two file formats available for Web pages: GIF and JPEG. Each of these formats compresses the file in a different way, and each format is best for a different type of image. JPEGs (Joint Photographic Experts Group) are best for photographic images. GIF files are good for images like cartoons and simple graphics that have large areas of similar colours. We'll try both formats.

Paint Shop Pro has a very simple method of optimising images for the World Wide Web.

Tip:

Most people that log onto the web have screen resolutions of 1024 pixels wide and 768 pixels high. So a picture 600 pixels wide will take up over half the screen quite big enough to look at.

If you need a specific height, just type it in and the width will change automatically.

- To make sure the image is not too large, from the Image menu select Resize. Use the settings in figure 8.4.

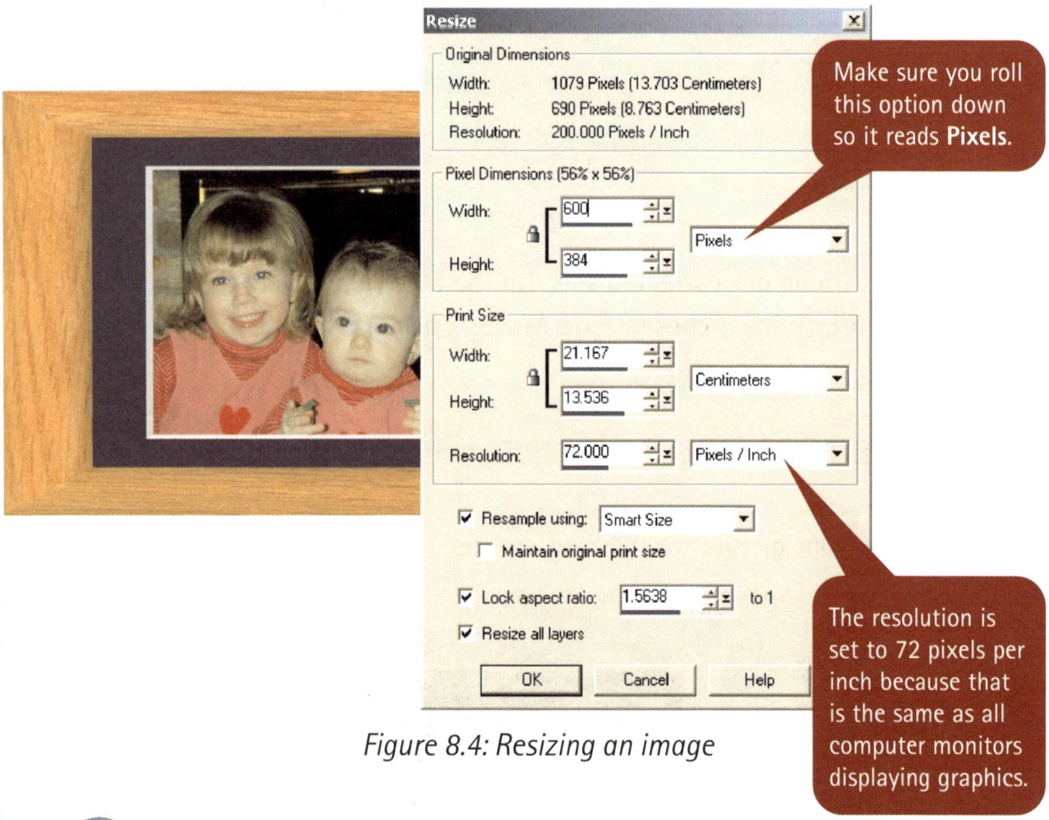

Figure 8.4: Resizing an image

- Change the width to 600 pixels wide and the height will change automatically to keep the proportions. Click OK.
- From the File menu select Export, JPEG Optimizer.

Here are the options that you are presented with.

Set the compression at about **50**. Try moving it to different values between 1 and 100, checking the difference in the Proofing window on the right. When you start to see the image breaking up you have gone too far.

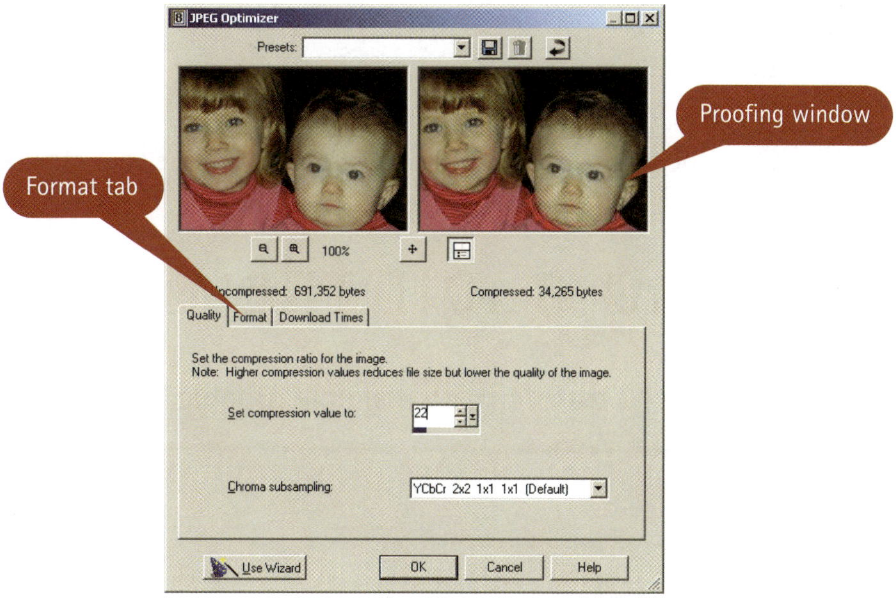

Figure 8.5

Click the **Format** tab.

As your image downloads you can have it display differently. I prefer the **Standard** style.

Press the **Download Times** bar.

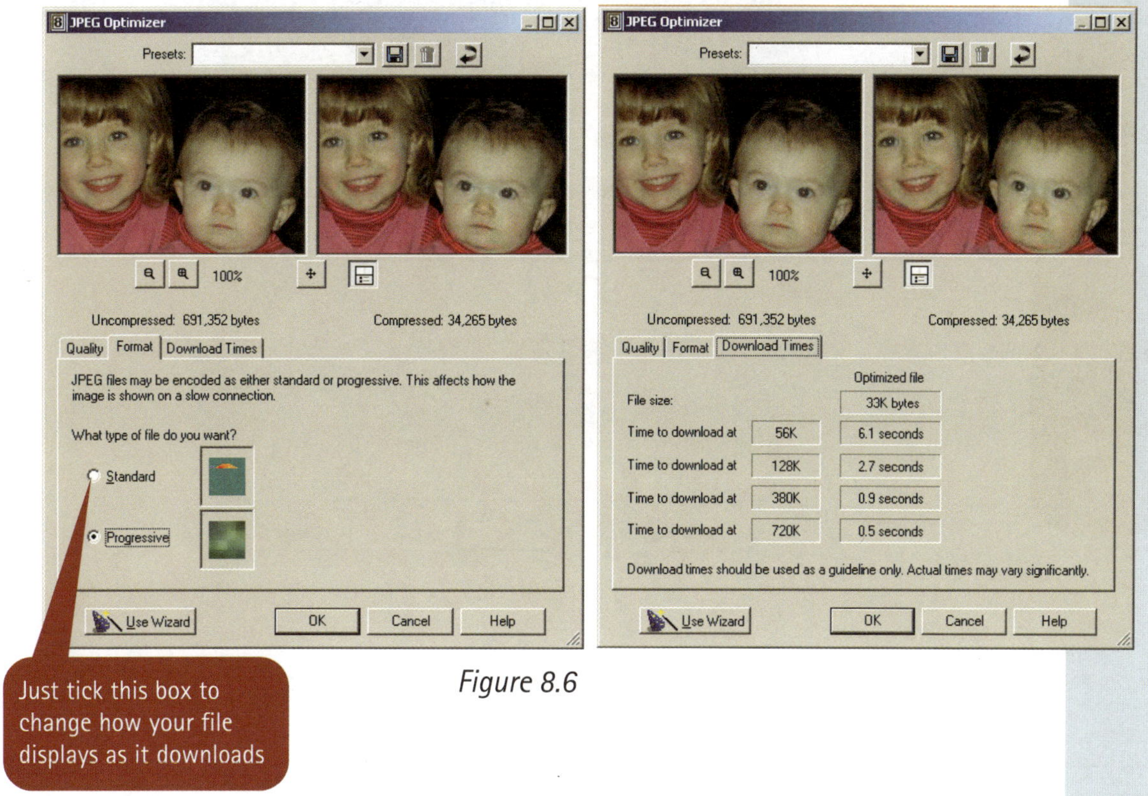

Figure 8.6

This window will show you the size of the file and how long it will take to download. Look at the file size of the uncompressed picture and then look at the compressed version - it really does make a huge difference.

- Press OK.
- Save the file and place it in a new folder for your web pictures.
- Close the original retouched picture but don't save your changes.

Creating a .gif file

Finally, we'll look at transforming a simple graphic to a GIF format file suitable for the Web.

- Open your vector Submarine.
- From the Image menu select Resize and make this image 600 pixels wide.
- Next, from the File menu select Export, GIF Optimizer.

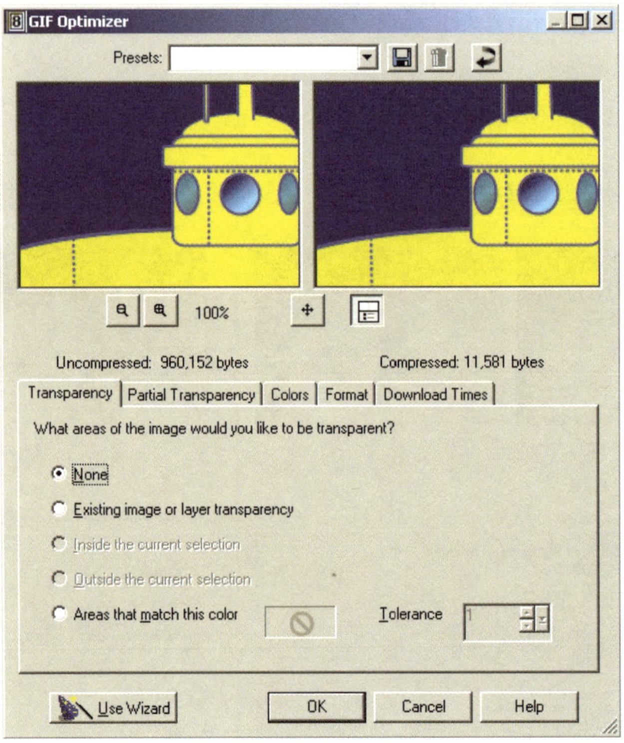

Figure 8.7

Tip:

If you want to make part of your picture transparent, click **Areas that match this colour**. A picker icon will appear. Click the colour you need to be transparent, such as the blue background, and it will disappear.

- Don't worry about Partial Transparency. Click Colors.

Because there is a colour gradation in the Submarine windows we will only be able to take a few colours away; if there were no graduations you could reduce the number of colours right down and make the file size much smaller.

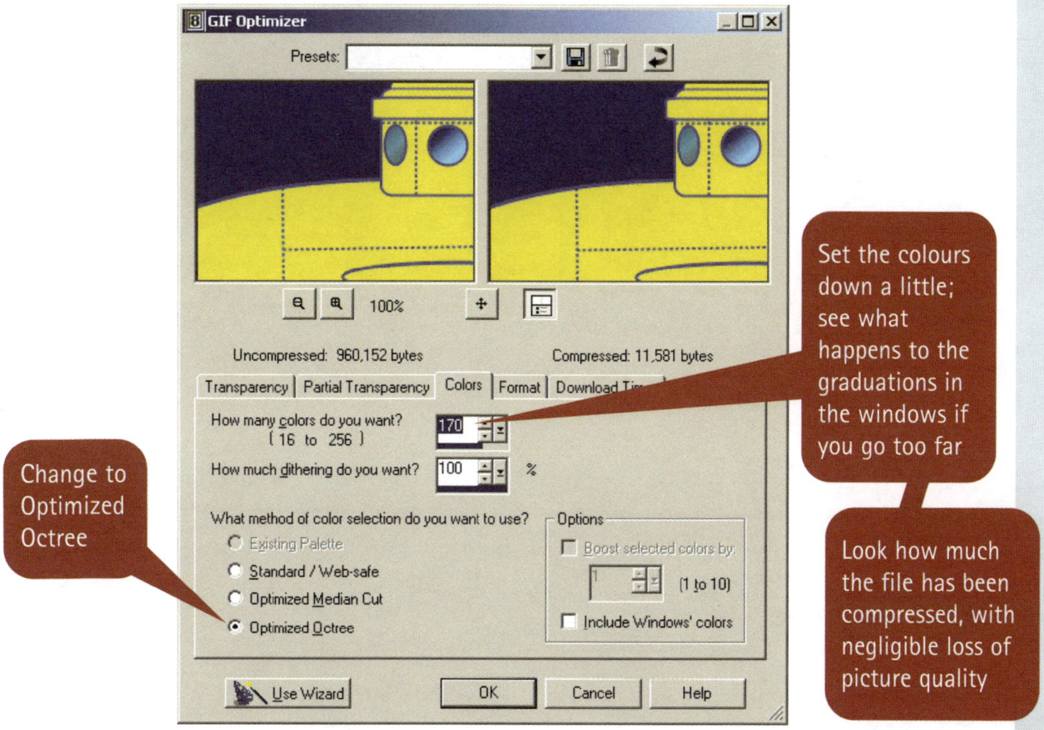

Figure 8.8: gif optimiser colours

- Check the **Format** and **Download Times** as you did before for the **RedEye** picture.
- Click **OK** and save.

Well, I think a career in digital art should be right around the corner!

Index